Giants

Giants

Nigel Marven

HarperCollins*Publishers*

77–85 Fulham Palace Road

London W6 8JB

The HarperCollins website address is:

www.**fire**and**water**.com

05 04 03 02 01 00 99

10 9 8 7 6 5 4 3 2 1

© 1999 Nigel Marven

For my mother who encouraged my passion for wild creatures and my father who made me realise nothing was impossible

ISBN 0 00 220157 7

Originated, printed and bound in Great Britain by The Bath Press

Contents

6   **Foreword**

10

Snakes

30

Sharks

56

Bears

82

Lizards

100

Birds

126

Tarantulas

142   **Species index**

Foreword

As a little boy I was never interested in train sets or Meccano, instead I'd have races with stick insects along the washing line, and have my breath taken away by the simple excitement of catching my first great crested newt. Wild animals were my passion and only interest. My parents thought it was a phase I was going through but I'm now 38 and three-quarters and it's far from over.

After studying botany/zoology at Bristol University, I even made it my career. I have been a producer of wildlife documentaries for 14 years now, and even when things go wrong and it seems that completing the film is an impossible task (you always do in the end), I still have to pinch myself that I'm doing the job that I do.

The series *Giants* is my first time in front of the camera, but other than the fact I have to talk into that glass eye, I am not doing anything really different to what I have always done, squelching through swamps, climbing trees, poking about in holes and crawling around on my belly in an attempt to get myself and the camera team up close and personal to wild creatures.

I hope I am useful in another way too. If you are doing a series about giant animals, you need a way to judge scale, and for this series that something is me. On the one hand with our specialised lenses we can make a beetle look as big as a dinosaur. On the other hand the colossal size of whale sharks, which are nearly as big as dinosaurs, means nothing on screen if there isn't a swimmer in the same frame to compare it to.

Many big creatures have a fearsome reputation too, but I hoped to get across that they deserve respect, perhaps even admiration rather than fear and loathing. With minimal risk I walked with wild bears and snorkelled with white sharks. I couldn't have done either of those things if they'd lived up to their reputation of being malicious and malevolent towards people.

Initially I was worried that connoisseurs of natural history programmes and books, would regard giant animals as a subject that was too simple to be interesting, but the more I delved into the world of giants, the more surprises I found. I had no idea that there were sharks over 6.4 m (21 ft) long living under the polar ice cap. Could one of my favourite birds, the bizarre marabou stork, really be a contender for the land bird with the greatest wing span? Andean condors were another. I had read somewhere that there was a unique fiesta honouring them in Peru. If polar bears become giants to endure the cold because animals with a large surface to volume ratio conserve heat more effectively, then what benefit was there for tropical pythons and boas to become the massive predators that they are?

To find out the answers, I joined film crews all over the world travelling to 15 countries in six continents, flying 240,000 km (150,000 miles), and between temperatures of 30°C (90°F) to minus 30°C (minus 22°F). The year I have spent coming eyeball-to-eyeball with giants has been a dream come true. I hope you enjoy the series and this book as much as I've enjoyed producing and writing them.

Acknowledgements

A natural history series and book of this kind owe their genius to a huge number of people. I'm particularly indebted to the core production team of Bill Butt, Colin Collis, Conrad Maufe, Emma Mansfield, Martin Parker and Imogen Sparks, they've all worked incredibly hard. As has Dave McCormick who edited all six films in this series and who encouraged this first-time presenter with his constant enthusiasm. I owe a huge debt of gratitude to every single cameraman, all of whom have sweated blood and tears to get into positions where they've used their technical skills and supreme creativity for beautiful, and often spectacular shots. Soundmen Mark Roberts and Roger Long have accompanied me on some very arduous expeditions and kept me going with their constant good humour as well as collecting marvellous sound that captures the atmosphere of our adventures. I must also thank the scientists and naturalists that work with giant creatures who have all been so generous in sharing their knowledge and expertise. My thanks to all those whose names appear in the text of the book, but I must also mention Graham Thompson in Australia; Mark Dumas in Canada; Terri Gover, John and Kathleen Hancock and Mark Ormond in England; Wahyu Hindarto in Indonesia; Gunnar Engblom in Peru; Bernardo Zilletti in Spain; Dean Henderson in Thailand; and William Moller in Uganda. Thanks also to the team at HarperCollins: Katie Piper the editor who did her magic on my words, Victoria Alers-Hankey who typed up uninterpretable scrawl faxed from far-flung corners of the world, Claire Marsden the assistant editor, and publishing director Myles Archibald who enthused about *Giants* from the beginning. Last but not least, thanks to my wife Jenny for putting up with my long stints away from home, and for all her support.

Production credits

Controller of Network Programming for United Productions-HTV West Tom Archer
Executive Producer Rob MacIver
Director Bill Butt
Researchers Colin Collis, Conrad Maufe
Field Assistant Martin Parker
Production Co-ordinator Emma Mansfield
Production Secretary Imogen Sparks
Unit Manager Christine Ward
Music Paul Hardcastle
Sound Recordists Mark Roberts, Roger Long, Trevor Gosling, Jeremy Ashton
Film Editing David McCormick
Dubbing Editor Angela Groves
Dubbing Mixers Graham Wild, Chris Domaille
Photography Neil Bromhall, Rod Clarke, Jeff Goodman, Nick Hayward, Malcolm Ludgate, Mark Payne-Gill, Mike Pitts, Rick Price, Ian Salvage, Martin Saunders, Gavin Thurston, Mark Yates

Snakes

The world's largest snakes belong to the python and boa families. These snakes are not venomous and instead kill their prey by constriction, gradually tightening their muscular coils until the life is squeezed from the victim's body. The largest snakes can kill prey up to the size of domestic livestock. When you have had the chance to see these massive snakes close up this fact comes as no surprise.

THE MONSTROUS REPTILE SLID FROM THE BANK INTO THE RIVER. WHETHER the plunging giant was a crocodile or a snake made little difference, either way it would make short work of the distance between it and Tarzan. A titanic struggle would follow, Tarzan and his attacker would spin in the water. Would he be drowned, swallowed or bitten clean in half? Of course not. With his last breath, using every ounce of his strength, Tarzan would either stab or strangle his scaly opponent.

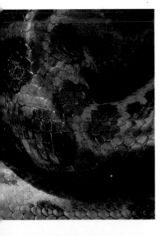

I used to adore those Hollywood jungle adventures. I realised early on however, that while the film makers were factually accurate in terms of the species of crocodiles they used, they took great liberties with the geographical distribution, size and capabilities of the snakes concerned. Tarzan came from Africa, the home of the Nile crocodile, so an attack by one of these could definitely be a possibility. But when he struggled inside the coils of a snake, the species used in the films was either an anaconda or a boa constrictor, both of which are only found in the New World. These two snakes have a legendary reputation, often portrayed as predators of people, but only the anaconda is massive enough actually to do this and in reality attacks are rare.

The term 'boa constrictor' is sometimes used in a broad sense simply meaning a huge snake, but the *Boa constrictor* is the scientific name for the common boa, a grey or silver snake with saddles of brown along the back which becomes brick red or even crimson towards the tail, a distinct species found in central and southern areas of South America. In fact, this particular species doesn't even make the top five biggest snakes which are the reticulated python, the amethystine python, the green anaconda, the Indian python and the African rock python.

Even though it is noticeably smaller than the other five – over most of its range the common boa rarely exceeds 3 m (10 ft) – in snake terms this is still large. There are approximately 2,700 species of snake in the world and surprisingly only seven regularly reach or exceed 5.5 m (18 ft) in length. The maximum size of exceptional common boas is somewhere between 5.5–5.8 m (18–19 ft), the same as the longest venomous snake, the king cobra, although the body of the latter is much more slender. All other snakes fall far behind these giants and lesser giants, and only a dozen or so attain a length of 3.6 m (12 ft), although some of these, Africa's gaboon viper for example, are so heavy they outweigh some longer snakes.

All of the really big snakes belong to the family Boidae, the pythons and boas. There are 27 and 35 species in each family respectively. They are regarded as primitive snakes still showing affinities to the ancestral snake stock. It is thought that the prototype originated from a lizard or lizard-like reptile. All boas and pythons have skeletons with the vestiges of a pelvic girdle, and outside their body there are spurs at the base of the tail, the remnants of hind legs that atrophied during evolution. They also have two well-developed lungs, more advanced snakes only have one, which represents a more efficient use of of space in a long, narrow body. Boas and pythons have small, irregularly-arranged head scales, not the large plates or shields of more advanced snakes.

All boas and pythons kill their prey by constriction. Hollywood's depiction of Tarzan fighting for his life wrapped in muscular reptilian coils was exactly right. I've seen other feature films where medium-sized boas or pythons have been given roles as venomous snakes, but in fact they never have a poisonous bite. When hunting they strike using their 100 or so inwardly-curved teeth to tear through flesh like saw blades. Once they have a grip, they throw a series of neat coils about the body of their prey, inexorably tightening the embrace and applying even pressure from all directions every time the trapped animal tries to breathe. The prey's bones are rarely broken – it is suffocated rather than crushed to death. There are other snakes that also use this technique, such as king snakes, rat snakes and European whip snakes. Even venomous species whose prime method for incapacitating prey is to hijack its body with toxic chemicals, sometimes use their weight to immobilise their catch.

Squeezing the last breath from their prey is a strategy that is unique to snakes. It is an elegant solution for a predator without arms or legs which could be at a disadvantage when compared to other hunters that can run and jump. In fact, snakes are extremely successful and are found in all of the Earth's major ecosystems except at the north and south poles. The way snakes subdue prey is extraordinary, but given that they have teeth that pierce rather than cut, the next phase of the feeding process is awe-inspiring.

Left, These baby common boas (*Boa constrictor*) can reach 4 m (13 ft) in length. They bear live young with litters of up to 50 at a time. They are found in the wild in south and central America and some islands in the West Indies

Top left, From baby snakes to giant ones. Green anacondas appeared in the Tarzan films as the hero's deadly attacker. Although in his native country of Africa he would never actually have encountered one – they are found in South America

Burmese Python

I owned my first python when I was 14 years old. It was a Burmese python, one of the five biggest snakes. A gorgeous creature, boldly marked with an intricate pattern of irregular brown blotches on a yellow background, with a dark marking in the shape of an arrowhead on the top of its head. In the wild these pythons can exceed 6.1 m (20 ft) in length, well-fed captives can grow much larger. The Burmese python comes from southern Asia, and its range extends from Pakistan in the west to southern China in the east, and south to the Malay archipelago. It also ranges further north than any other giant snakes. The 'hibernating' pythons of the Bharatpur Reserve in India are famous. The snakes remain torpid within the burrows of porcupines, and the reptiles and mammals may even share a tunnel, apparently showing no interest or aggression towards each other.

Given the right conditions – a heated, spacious and strong vivarium, a regular supply of rodents when small, and rabbits, fowl, or even pigs when adult – this species of snake does very well in captivity. There is no need for the food to be alive, in fact in the United Kingdom it is illegal to give live prey to captive snakes; well-thawed mice and rats from the freezer are just as acceptable.

For the first six months of its life my python was fed twice a week and a meal could be one, two or three mice depending on how hungry it was. Then it graduated on to half-grown rats, and by the end of its first year, it could eat large adult ones. It could have easily been sustained completely on mice as its body grew; 15 mice have the same nutritional value as 3–4 rats. However snakes do need to give their jaws a proper workout, and without this I would have ended up with a large-bodied snake with a disproportionately tiny head. This would certainly not have been a natural state of affairs. Giant pythons and boas attain such a massive size in order to exploit large prey species, otherwise unavailable to

other snakes, thereby avoiding competition for food resources. To achieve a head able to cope with really prodigious meals, there is a record of a 6 m (20 ft) Burmese python swallowing a leopard, they have to start eating larger packages from a relatively early age.

Adult pythons can eat meals that are 95 per cent of their body weight – one 37 kg (82 lb) python killed and ate a 35 kg (77 lb) impala. My python would begin any

Above, This albino form of the Burmese python is also known as the 'golden python'. The markings are the same as the Burmese python except that the dark blotches on the back are yellow and the background is white

Left, Burmese pythons are boldly marked with brown blotches on a yellow background

spectacular feeding feat by searching for the head of the rodent, then it would swiftly open its jaws and engage its teeth. Usually the food was several times larger than the python's own head and much wider than its narrow neck, and it was astounding that in 20 minutes or so (up to an hour if the size of the meal approached the snake's maximum gape) the food would disappear inside the reptile.

This vanishing act is achieved by the extraordinary flexibility and elasticity of the python's head and skull. The brain case is solid bone, this vulnerable area needs protection from the kicks of struggling prey, but otherwise the skull is held together by flexible joints rather than solid bone connections. The two halves of each jaw are only loosely connected and can move independently. The teeth are actually on moveable struts and if I watched closely I could see how my python moved its jaws backward and forwards, and even from side to side, jiggling the food into a suitable position for swallowing. Slowly it walked its jaws forward, the teeth are alternatively freed and refastened, dragging the food towards the gullet. Getting past the rodent's shoulders was the most difficult task because that is the widest part of any animal and one of the reasons we are rarely on the menu of even the largest snakes. The breadth of our shoulders makes us too much of a mouthful. Once my python had overcome that obstacle, it distorted its head even more to pull it around and over the meal. When eating prey head first, the animal's legs tend to fold back against the body. If a python started from the other end, the limbs could bend back and stick out, making the parcel more difficult to swallow and increasing the risk of the snake being injured by the sharp claws of its prey.

The bulge of the rodent stretched the snake's neck to such a degree that each individual scale became an island surrounded by elastic blue skin – it is astonishing that nothing tears. The lump now moved through the distended neck, powerful muscles forcing it towards the stomach. Snakes don't have a breast bone so the tips of the ribs splay apart to accommodate large meals. Powerful digestive juices would begin working immediately, but the meal would be noticeable inside my python for the next two or three days. Without teeth to grind up food like us, digestion must proceed from scratch but eventually the bones and connective tissue dissolve and the body inside liquefies.

Pampered with all the food they can eat, Burmese pythons grow rapidly in captivity. Babies are about 50 cm (20 in) long; within two years they can be 2.4–3 m (8–10 ft) long and weigh 14 kg (30 lb). In the town of Gurnee Mills near Chicago, Illinois, I visited Baby, a Burmese python, and the largest snake in captivity. Even though she fasts in the winter time, for 3–6 months every year she is so massive that it takes ten people to hold her. She is 8.5 m (27 ft 10 in) long. In the spring she is at her lowest weight of 152 kg (335 lb) but then she begins feeding, consuming a chicken, turkey or duck every fortnight, putting on another 45 kg (100 lb) by the summer. Because of their pleasing pattern and tractable disposition, Burmese pythons are a favourite with showmen and pet keepers all over the world, so they have probably been seen by more people than any other giant snake.

They breed readily in captivity, producing clutches of up to 100 eggs. There is a ready market for the babies, and pet Burmese snakes are growing rapidly in popularity. Keeping these powerful creatures is not to be taken lightly, however, since even docile ones that have been around people since hatching are potentially dangerous once they reach 3 m (10 ft) in length. In July 1993, a 15 year old boy in Commerce City, Colorado was attacked and killed by a 3.3 m (11 ft) Burmese python. In 1997 a 19 year old man was killed in New York City while preparing to feed his 4 m (13 ft) Burmese.

Fatalities and attacks by captive pythons should be kept in perspective. There are tens of thousands of these snakes in the world and there have only been a handful of attacks. Large domestic dogs have killed many more people than large snakes. By taking a few simple precautions, accidents with pythons shouldn't

Above, Slowly and meticulously the snake works the rabbit inside; here it has now almost entirely disappeared. You can see the way in which the rabbit has distended the body of the snake. Powerful digestive juices will now get to work breaking down the rabbit

Left, The way a snake feeds is an extraordinary process. Here you can see how wide the snake has to open the two halves of its jaw to work the rabbit into its mouth. The shoulders – the widest part of the body – are the most difficult

happen at all. No one should attempt to handle a large snake (2.4 m (8 ft) or more) by themselves, as a rule of thumb one person is needed for every 1.5 m (5 ft) of snake. The coils of a large snake should never be allowed around your neck or torso. The first reaction of a startled or frightened constrictor is to tighten its grip. This can do more than spoil your weekend especially if a vulnerable part is enveloped and there isn't someone around to unravel it.

Precautions should also be taken at feeding time. Most pythons are eager feeders and can strike and constrict potential prey that is obviously too big for them to swallow. Their eyesight is not good and they rely heavily on scent to identify prey. If you have been handling rabbits or chickens, or have just stroked a cat or dog before feeding a snake, the smell could trigger a feeding response, and you could be unconscious or even dead before the snake loosens its grip. Mistaken attacks can be avoided if you wash your hands thoroughly with soap before handling a python and try to avoid getting the scent of prey on your clothing.

Of course boas and pythons in the wild are an entirely different proposition. Given the chance, they will slither away unnoticed, but if provoked or caught they will strike aggressively. Until the filming of *Giants* began I had only seen one species of giant snake in nature, the amethystine python, a denizen of the rain forests of Papua New Guinea and Northern Australia. While looking for frogs in northern Queensland on a damp night, the light of my lantern flicked across a

'vine' that reflected the light in a way that wasn't quite right. When the 'vine' moved I realised it was a snake and a reasonably large one at that. The reptile hung from a branch with its prehensile tail. Its head seemed too large for its slender body and had large shield-like plates on the top. The snake's brown back had a series of large, grey-brown blotches arranged diagonally across it, and a wide grey-buff stripe along its sides. If the angle of my flashlight was just right its scales shone with a sheen of milky iridescence, the colour of amethyst, the feature that gives this python its name.

Moving slowly I approached within 2 m (6 ft). In this case this was about half a snake's length away. Close up the sheen on the scales was even more lustrous and this led me to believe that the snake had recently shed its skin. All snakes and lizards do this. Most lizards will lose theirs in small, ragged patches over a period of time, but snakes usually slough their whole outer covering in one go. The frequency with which this happens depends upon temperature, the snake's health – shedding may help dislodge blood-sucking ticks for example – how much food the snake has eaten, and how much it is growing. Young snakes slough more often because their growth rate is higher.

If I'd come across this python just before it was about to shed, its eyes would have been a milky grey from the fluid that forms between old and newly-formed skin. This fluid even gets in front of the eyes as the spectacle-like scales which cover them will also be replaced. Once the new skin is fully formed the python will rub its head against a branch or a rock until the old skin splits and rolls backwards inside-out, leaving the tail of the cast skin pointing in the direction of the departing snake. The amethystine python in front of me had such a shiny new skin it must have sloughed very recently; the constant wear and tear of pushing past leaves and branches means the skin quickly loses this high-gloss look.

With fluid grace the amethystine doubled back up its own body to the branch where its tail was anchored, disappearing into the foliage behind. This individual was about half the maximum size attained by this species. Amethystines are the longest snakes in Australia and can reach 8.5 m (28 ft) but are more frequently found at lengths of around 5 m (16 ft). For its length it is a slender python but it can still take prey as large as wallabies.

African Rock Python

There are three species of giant snake that approach or may even exceed 10 m (33 ft) in length. The African rock python, found on most of the African continent south of the Sahara is an example. In the wild their average size is probably 3–4 m (10–13 ft); old snakes can reach 6 m (19 ft) but they are not very common. A specimen shot at Bungerville on the Ivory Coast in 1932 is alleged to have been 9.8 m (32 ft) long but there was no official confirmation of this record. There are other reports of 9 m (30 ft) specimens from English naturalists Arthur Loveridge and George Lonsdale in the first half of the century. Both finds were in west Africa and both measurements were taken from the skins of freshly killed snakes. However, as skins can stretch or be stretched up to 25 per cent more than than their original length, verification of these reports is difficult.

I first looked for the African rock python in Uganda's Queen Elizabeth National Park. They are a tourist attraction there and sightings are virtually guaranteed. A ranger guided me through the Maramagumbo Forest in the early afternoon, the perfect time to see pythons basking in patches of leaf-filtered sun. The forest birds were quiet – most of their singing had been done in the relative cool of the morning – and the only sounds now were the contact calls of two black bee eaters which launched themselves from a twig above a pool to bathe. Dunking their bodies just beneath the surface they returned to their perch shaking the water droplets from their feathers. A patch of bright crimson on their throats flashed in the sunlight and feathers of a brilliant blue were intermingled with the black ones on their body. We followed the track further into the forest to a destination that could be heard long before we reached it. Soprano squeaks and squeals ran together as if they were static on a radio. A large bird with creamy-white wings negotiated the canopy above us, a palm nut vulture, one of the few vultures that can be vegetarian.

Some birds do subsist on the carbohydrate-packed fruits of oil palms, but this one used its hooked yellow bill to prey on the animals that were making the chittering noise ahead – it was fond of fruit bats.

The colony was under an arch of rock and this was a spectacular sight. The bats didn't just hang from the ceiling as you might expect. They jostled on the vertical sides of the arch too, and even in the gaps under the boulders on the floor. They were Egyptian fruit bats with faces covered in soft brown fur, like the faces of small dogs, except that no dog would have protruding brown eyes as huge as theirs. Some of the bats flew circuits between the two ends of the stone arch, flipping and turning on their translucent wings just before the rock wall that rushed towards them at the end of each lap; the precision of their flying is marvellous. Judging by the slick of black guano covering the boulders, the bats, thousands of them, have roosted under this natural rock bridge for many years. As a reliable food source they are a magnet for predators such as the vultures and the pythons. More often than not one or two snakes can be found there

Above, African rock pythons usually reach 3–4 m (10–13 ft) in the wild and may grow up to 5 m (16 ft) or more in captivity. They are brown or greenish-brown with irregular, dark brown markings running along the back and smaller spots on the sides

and if you are really fortunate – the ranger had seen it half a dozen times in as many months – you can watch a python swallowing a bat, but today there weren't even any loafing in the patches of dappled sun.

The Cameroon in west Africa is another hot spot for rock pythons, a country where, if you are not claustrophobic, you can crawl through narrow tunnels right into their lair. French photographer, Gilles Nicolet, spent two years working on this extraordinary story and he would be our advisor and most importantly introduce us to the snake hunters.

When we arrived wooden racks were covered with

strips of blackened meat and fish. A procession of large red ants tiptoed over the charred flesh. Their nest was in the tree from which the rack hung. The hunters had chosen this place because even though the ants would carry minuscule morsels of meat away, they would act as guard dogs, harrying away any flies before they could lay their eggs that would hatch into flesh-eating grubs. The smoking racks were strung high up to prevent the catch from being stolen by hyenas. The chocolate and brown hide of a roan and the smaller skin of a Buffon's kob, both species of antelope, were staked out in the sun. Gilles introduced me to the three

Left, The Gbaya tribe light fires when they are out on hunting trips. One of the reasons is that the ash-covered ground is a perfect medium for tracking, and a long continuous impression could lead to the most sought-after prize, the African rock python

hunters, Sambo and Adamou, two friends in their mid-forties, and Sambo's 22 year old son Abu. They belong to the Gbaya tribe and they hunt during the dry season, from November to March, and cultivate crops for the rest of the year. We were in the arid and empty province of Adamawa in Cameroon.

Gilles explained that the hunting party set up a bush camp like the one we had joined and then travelled up to 32 km (20 miles) a day hunting game. Once they had gathered enough to make it worthwhile, one of the party, usually the youngest, would take the smoked meat back to their village perhaps 161 km (100 miles) away.

To help them hunt they ignite bush fires. The reasons for this are fourfold. First, it is hard to see animals or their burrows if there is grass 3 m (10 ft) high, also the flames can flush out the game for the waiting hunters on the journey to the camp. We'd seen a singed cane rat, a huge rodent over 38 cm (15 in) long, a succulent meal, fleeing from a fire. Third, burning provides space and nutrients for the regrowth of new grass, fodder for next season's game, when the

Below, Armed just with a torch, all I could see ahead of me were Adamou's feet. After an initial bout of claustrophobia I followed him down through the tunnels to see if we could find the python in its lair

rainy season comes. Most of the trees have flame retardant bark and can survive this regime of seasonal burning. Finally, the ash-covered ground is a perfect medium for tracking, and a long continuous impression could lead to the most sought-after prize, the African rock python.

To the Gbaya tribe this is the king of snakes born from a dragon at the beginning of time. Catching a king is one of the most dangerous forms of hunting only undertaken by the most intrepid hunters. The tradition will probably perish very soon, because on the one hand large pythons are becoming rare. Gilles spent six months trailing Adamou, Sambo and Abu and in that time, they only found ten snakes over 3 m (10 ft) long. On the other hand, most of the younger men, the next generation of hunters, are too afraid to catch pythons. Adamou and Abu took me to the home of a python they had already tracked so I could find out why.

The burrows of aardvarks provide homes for many other animals in Africa. They live in grassland and their large ears allow them to hear hotspots of termite activity. Once they have located such a site they break into the insect's mound with their powerful front legs and sharp finger nails. Once the clay walls of a termite fortress are breached, the aardvark follows through with its long snout and sticky tongue and with these it feeds on little else but termites. Aardvarks with their strong legs and tough, durable hides, sparsely studded with stiff bristles, are excavators par excellence; they can dig labyrinths of burrow systems. In the Cameroon burrow systems may contain bats, monitor lizards, porcupines, water hogs, families of hyenas and even leopards, many of which, including the aardvark itself, you would not want to catch unawares.

As the python located by the hunters had made its home in an aardvark tunnel Adamou and Sambo checked carefully for tracks other than the slitherings of the snake as we approached its lair. To see the python we would have to crawl underground. Hunters have been buried alive by aardvarks that get a whiff of their scent. The mere geography of the tunnels also brings its own perils. If you are a novice and you wriggle forward down a steeply-sloping part of the burrow, unless there is a chamber large enough to turn around in up ahead, it is impossible to climb backwards up the slope – you are trapped. Adamou entered the burrow first and I followed but nearly withdrew before my feet had disappeared into the darkness. My mind was full of horrors and to move in the narrow corridor

you have to pull yourself along with your elbows with a light – a flashlight in my case, a flaming torch in Adamou's – stretched in front of you. I'd never experienced claustrophobia before but I did at that moment even though Adamou's feet were just ahead of me. After a few deep breaths I carried on, so great was my desire to see the python in its lair.

After about 5 m (16 ft) the tunnel split into two. Adamou crawled along the left fork allowing me to squeeze down the right one, which the hunters had

told me would soon open out into the python's chamber. I inched forward cautiously as African rock pythons have a reputation for being irritable and snappy. A flash of shiny scales glimmered in the torchlight. The python just about filled the chamber, the ophidian head that looked at me was the pinnacle of five looped coils. Their patterning was exquisite: spaced regularly along the python's body on a background of grey-brown, were islands of dark chocolate pigment with two-tone wavy margins of black then yellow. Some of the islands were splurges of yellow on the chocolate. Gilles told me that really old pythons lose their markings and become entirely black. The python was curious, and from the groove in the front of its mouth, its long forked tongue flicked out slowly, undulating gently in the air of the chamber. At close range and in the dark this was its main sense. In all snakes, the tongue is a device for gathering scent. Any chemicals in the air adhere to its moist surface, and these are then taken back into the mouth

Above, Once Adamou grabbed the snake from its burrow he put out his torch to try and keep it calm. In the pitch dark it took him over half an hour to drag the python to the surface and we were on hand to pull the snake into the light to be analysed by Jacobsen's organ, a specialised chemical sensor in the roof of the mouth. I was now only 1 m (3 ft) away so the python would also be able to perceive the heat of my body. Pythons and boas have a line of infra-red detectors along their upper lip. These heat sensors are not as sophisticated as those of pit vipers – rattlesnakes and their kin – but they do allow them to locate warm-blooded predators or prey in complete darkness. When I was further away the python would have detected the reverberations emanating from my wriggling body. All snakes are deaf to airborne sounds but the bones of the middle ear rest close to the jaw, so they can pick up any vibrations from the ground.

Gingerly I backed away from the python but my light must have flashed across its eyes. Nobody is sure why, but when chambers inhabited by snakes are completely dark they are much less likely to bite. In this case the illumination and movement made the snake strike towards me. Its head just fell short, thudding down onto the hard-packed soil. The gape of large pythons can be as wide as a tennis racket and they have about 100 razor-sharp, backward curving-teeth. I was so glad I didn't have to do what Adamou was about

to. After I'd cleared the tunnel Adamou entered the chamber. To protect himself from bites he had wrapped an antelope skin around his hand and forearm. Using the light from his flaming torch he found the python's head and grabbed it. In order to calm the snake he extinguished his torch and in the pitch dark it took him over half an hour to drag the python to the surface.

Now in the sunlight, I could really get a good idea of its size. From snakes I'd seen in captivity at home I estimated it was 4.5 m (15 ft) long, half the size of the Bungerville specimen, but still impressive. The girth of the snake was the same as the thickest part of my leg. This width suggested that the snake was a gravid female; in all boas and pythons females are proportionately heavier than males, particularly when carrying a clutch of eggs or a litter of babies. In giant snakes there is also a disproportionate increase in stockiness with an increase in length. If she reaches 6 m (19 ft) this python will have the girth of my waist which is 86 cm (34 in)!

The Cameroonian hunters slapped her body repeatedly with the flat of their hands, a practice that in their experience has a calming effect on the snake. After a while she did seem to lose her fight and her

Below, We stretched the snake along the ground to see how long it really was. I estimated it was 4.5 m (15 ft) long, an impressive size for an African rock python in the wild

muscular coils hung limply. A snake of this size is worth about US$35 to the hunters. To kill the reptile they would usually slit its throat leaving the skin undamaged, although the meat is the most valuable part of the snake, exactly three-quarters of its worth. Of course we released the snake back into its burrow and I reimbursed the hunters for the money they had lost.

This snake was probably 20 years old. Stuffed with food and kept at optimum temperatures, African rock pythons in captivity can reach maturity and a size of 2.5 m (8 ft) in 3–5 years. The vagaries and hardships of the wild – the dry season, a dearth of game and being loaded with energy-sapping ticks, mites and worms – mean that growth is a much more demanding process. Maturing females in particular have an even harder time. The one we had caught probably hadn't fed for 1–2 months, she cannot afford to catch or swallow prey in case she damages the eggs developing inside her.

After laying a clutch of up to 80 eggs in the seclusion of the aardvark burrow she would then coil around them and fast for even longer, not feeding or even drinking for another 60 days until the eggs hatch. Python eggs are a valuable delicacy and if the hunters find an incubating python they check the condition of the clutch. If the eggs are white, and their parchment-like shells are not too crumpled and battered, they are edible as their development has probably not gone too far. If the eggs are stained with soil and crumpled in places it means they've been developing for weeks rather than days; they get dirty every time the female leaves them to bask in the sun, and they crumple as the developing embryos use up the yolk inside. The hunters know eggs with crenulated, dirty shells will give them embryonic replicas of adult pythons 60 cm (24 in) long, rather than liquid ingredients for fried eggs or an omelette.

All pythons lay eggs. The females of the giant pythons and several Australian species coil around them to protect them from predators and more curiously from getting chilled. How can a creature that relies on external sources of heat do this? Some leave their burrow to bask in the sun, returning later with solar-heated bodies to raise the temperature of their clutch. Others, particularly pythons that are found in cooler climates, for example, at higher altitudes in the tropics, or more northerly parts of Australia, 'shiver' to warm their eggs; their bulky muscles twitch and spasm

generating metabolic heat. This raises the temperature of the clutch by 9°C (18°F) during the day even when cloudy and by 18°C (36°F) in the cool of the night. At the end of incubation females can lose 15 per cent of their body weight because of the increased metabolic rate when they shiver.

The female python's maternal instincts wane as soon as the babies begin hatching. Within hours the mother loses interest in her offspring and leaves them to fend for themselves. The snakelings slice through the papery egg shells, using a tooth on their snouts, just like the egg tooth of birds this drops off a day or two. Left to their own devices, they must hunt instinctively, but before they do that they shed their skins.

Above, Into the coils of death. Compare the width of my neck to the girth of the snake. African rock pythons will kill and eat crocodiles. Fortunately today I was not on the menu!

Reticulated Python

So now I'd seen a giant python caught in the wild and I was ready to try to do it myself, a species of snake that is probably the longest in the world seemed a good starting point. The reticulated python approaches and may even exceed 9 m (30 ft). It is a snake of the humid tropics of Asia, found in Burma, Indo China, the Malay Peninsula, and on most of the region's islands including the Indonesian archipelago and the Philippines. This python's swimming abilities help it colonise far-flung islands; it was one of the first land animals to return to Krakatoa in Indonesia after the island was blown apart and then buried in ash by the colossal volcanic eruption of 1883.

My search started in Singapore. It would be understandable for you to assume that I would have little hope of finding one in a bustling city, but within reason, reticulated pythons adapt well to living in densely-populated regions. As long as they have some cover they can make an easy living picking off rats, hens, dogs and even pigs. They were frequent in the Thai capital of Bangkok at the turn of the century, and a 6 m (20 ft) specimen was found under a stable in the middle of the city. Malcolm Smith, an English physician and highly-accomplished amateur herpetologist reported them there 30 years later. A doctor at the Royal Court of Siam, he reported one entering the gardens of the palace and eating a Siamese cat belonging the royal family. In the 1990s they were still found within the city limits of Bangkok even though it is now bustling and over-populated with notorious air pollution problems. Reticulated pythons have been in the news in Singapore too. There were seven documented python encounters in 1997 and 1998. These included a snake lunging out of a toilet bowl to bite a golfer who was sitting on it. Fortunately no major damage was done. On another occasion a 5 m (16 ft) python lay across the path of Mr Henrik Nybom as he went for his early morning jog in a city park.

When Mr Lee Yoong Kum opened the bonnet of his car he found a python wrapped around the engine, presumably warming itself up. The Café Flora in Orchard Road had an unusual guest; a 3 m (10 ft) python, first spotted near the entrance of the open air restaurant, then slithered into a pipe. The hotel staff attempted to entice the snake out with raw meat and eggs; they then tried smoke and water but it still wouldn't budge. The police arrived but were unable to find it. Finally, a pest control company managed to force it out from its retreat by spraying it with formalin. It was then put into a sack and was taken to a zoo. In Singapore, there is so much building work, for motorways in particular, that most of the python's natural cover is being destroyed, which is why they are being seen in the open more frequently.

My reticulated python was in a monsoon drain at the side of Buona Vista tube station on Commonwealth Avenue West. It was 10 pm and the reptile was coiled at the shadowy entrance of a tunnel where the drain went under a busy road. Lifting its head it hissed sibilantly when we approached. Jonathan Kung, curator of the Jurong Reptile Park, and some of his keepers were here to help me. The rule of thumb about having one handler for every 1.5 m (5 ft) of snake applies to tame individuals and rises to one person for every 1 m (3 ft) with a wild python that is nervous and aggressive. We

Below, Probably the longest snake in the world the reticulated python can grow to 9 m (30 ft) or more. It can be found in Burma, Indo China, the Malay Peninsula, and on most of the region's islands including the Indonesian archipelago and the Philippines

estimated that this individual was over 5 m (16 ft) long. There were four of us so we didn't quite make the equation. At least Jonathan and his team were experienced in this sort of thing, It was noticeable how far back the camera crew were positioned, they said they'd move in closer when I had secured the python's head.

I am left-handed so I wrapped a hessian towel around my right hand; this would give the snake a target if he chose to strike at me giving me a chance to grab it gently and firmly behind the head. The filming lights were switched on and I could see the python clearly. Even so, the patterns on its body are difficult to describe: rich yellow and jet black interwoven with different shades of brown, highlights in the folds of the body shimmered with iridescence like oil on water. This was a handsome snake indeed, it was also a very irascible one.

As I approached its head 1 m (3 ft) of body launched away from the coils. The open mouth hit my towel with a thud. I had to be fast; I didn't want the snake to damage the sensitive inside of its mouth and get its teeth enmeshed in the weave of the material. It could lose them if we had to prise it off. I reached out with my left hand and grabbed it around the neck, the reptile loosened its grip in surprise, letting go of the towel. I gripped it close to the base of its head so it couldn't swing round to bite me. Jonathan and the others ran in to grab the bulk of the python's body. I had caught my first giant snake.

Green Anaconda

The reticulated python competes for its place as the longest snake with the green anaconda of South America. A report in 1944 attributes a length of 11.5 m (38 ft) for this New World species. This record stems from a specimen shot by a group of oil workers near the upper reaches of the Orinoco River in eastern Colombia. The reptile was measured with a surveyors tape then the men left for a while. On their return the snake had vanished. Was the anaconda really that long? As with all these old records nobody will ever know for sure.

Based on snakes that have been caught in the wild and made their way into zoological collections, or snakes that have been grown from babies, it would seem that there are many more reticulated pythons greater than 6 m (20 ft) than anacondas of this length. However, this may be because large reticulated pythons are easier to come by in the wild and are easier to maintain and grow in captivity, or perhaps lengthy anacondas are just very rare. There's no dispute that the anaconda attains weights greater than other serpents though; a 5 m (17 ft) specimen is as heavy as a 7 m (24 ft) reticulated python. They are found in South America, east of the Andes mountains: Colombia, Venezuela, Guyana, French Guiana, Ecuador, Peru, Brazil, Paraguay and Bolivia. The island of Trinidad has them too.

Since childhood I've dreamt of seeing them in their natural habitat and filming for *Giants* I hoped to fulfil this dream. I travelled to Caracas, the capital of Venezuela and then made a short trip in a light plane to the small town of San Fernando. I was now in the heart of the Llanos, a 300,000 sq. km (116,000 sq. miles) savannah (one third of Venezuela's territory) that floods from prolonged heavy rain from June to November. Usually between December and May the watery sheet recedes leaving a plain of cracked mud and a few small pools. In March, the year I was there, this wasn't the case. My heart sank as I drove to my final destination, the 800 sq. km (309 sq. miles) of

cattle ranch of El Frio, there were vast lakes on both sides of the road, by this time these should have receded. The anaconda biologists Jésus Rivas and his wife Renee had asked us to film at this time because the anacondas would be concentrated in whatever water was remaining. Would the aquatic giants be impossible to find in these vast lakes?

The crew had been filming scenic shots and general Llanos wildlife for two days before I arrived but they hadn't found a single large snake. We'd start early the next day and search for more. Tired from the long journey, I fell into a fitful sleep, my semi-conscious thoughts were full of giant anacondas. I willed us to find one, not just because of the filming, but because I'd always wanted to.

Just after dawn we headed out along one of the

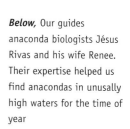

Below, Our guides anaconda biologists Jésus Rivas and his wife Renee. Their expertise helped us find anacondas in unusually high waters for the time of year

elevated dirt roads that bisected the ranch. Jésus thought our best chance was a shallow lake on the eastern perimeter. It was still a big area to cover but anacondas had recently been seen there basking on the banks. This location was one the Tarzan film-makers would have approved of. Sunbathing next to the water were hundreds of caiman, a South American crocodile, that grows to about 2 m (6 ft) or so. If our vehicle carried on at the same speed they didn't move, their toothy jaws agape to lose heat by evaporation from the fleshy soft insides of their mouth. If we slowed down or stopped they slid cleanly into the water just like in the films. Sometimes the caimans shared their basking spot with freshwater turtles, the size and shape of dinner plates.

About half of the flat land was still under the water, which took on the blue of the sky and contrasted with the emerald green of the plants which appeared above the water. Huge flocks of whistling ducks swirled from one feeding spot to another. There were groups of ibis too; glossy ibis were the most common but there was also a scarlet variety which glowed incandescent red against the jade vegetation.

This was a land of giants: statuesque black and white jabiru storks with multicoloured beaks like broad swords, the world's tallest birds. Herds of capybara galloped, bounded or swam ahead of us, the largest rodents on earth, weighing 68 kg (150 lb) and standing 1.2 m (4 ft) at the shoulder. They are a favourite prey of the bigger anacondas. On that day I also saw my first

giant anteater, and what a brilliant animal it was, curled up asleep using its tail as a duvet. At first it was hard to make out which end was which, but then it sensed our approach and unwound. At the front end there was a pair of small black eyes at the base of an inordinately long snout; after that came a brindled body with a long broad black stripe and a thin white one along each side. This was carried by four stocky black legs armed with claws like grappling hooks for tearing apart termite mounds so that long snout containing an even longer, sticky tongue could probe inside and lap up the insects. For me the highlight was its tail, a long fluffy banner that trailed behind it as it ran. About as long as I am tall, and weighing up to 39 kg (86 lb), the anteater appeared clumsy, but I could only jog alongside for a while, before it sprinted away.

We arrived at the lake where anacondas had been reported which wasn't as big as I had expected. On the far shore cattle appeared like part of a mirage; currents of warm air rose and wobbled in front of them distorting their shapes. Without any kind of shade, this was going to be hot work.

Jésus discarded his shoes and socks and showed us the technique he uses to find anacondas. As he stepped into the water he instructed us to take pigeon steps so as not to step right over them, and to feel for anything that seemed firmer than the squelchy morass of mud, leaves and water plants. As we felt our way with the toes or the soles of the feet, we were told that something firm could be the compact muscles of a

Above, While it may not be the longest species of snake, the green anaconda is certainly the heaviest – a 5 m (17 ft) specimen is as heavy as a 7 m (24 ft) reticulated python. It is olive-brown or greenish-yellow with regular dark ovals on its back

coiled snake. He warned us to look ahead in case there was a movement in the water or an island of gleaming scales above it. There were hazards: small aquatic insects with a painful bite, freshwater sting rays with poisonous spines in their tails that can cause an excruciating wound, and caimans. However, if you stepped on the latter, the reptile would merely explode away from right under your feet in a cascade of muddy water, frightening you out of your skin, but not biting which at least was a blessing.

For over four hours we squelched around. Jésus, his wife Renee, Mark Yates the cameraman, and Emma Munsfield the production assistant; wherever we waded others waded too. There were no other humans but scores of wattled jacanas, a species of lily trotter. This bird has a dull red wattle hanging down on either side of the beak, a black head and neck contrasting with a chestnut body. When they flew or flicked their wings, which they did all the time raising them above their heads as if to semaphore, their yellow primary feathers made the contrast even greater. Lightweight with spindly legs and long, splayed toes, they could stand on the floating vegetation rather than wading through the water which contained the insects, sting rays and anacondas.

These birds can fall prey to anacondas; the snakes lie just beneath the surface with only their nostrils visible to enable them to breathe. If a lily trotter teeters within range the snake strikes. In a split second it cleaves the surface of the water to embed as many of its teeth into the bird as it can. Once the snake has a firm grip the prey is dragged under the water. The anaconda throws a coil or two around the body although constriction is hardly necessary because the bird drowns. Depending upon the size of the snake, a whole range of animals – ducks and other birds, capybara and other mammals coming down to drink, ranging in size from rats to deer and even caiman – can be caught unawares using this technique. Unfortunately, our probing toes didn't surprise any anacondas and my worries about finding them continued through that night too.

The next day we started again quartering the same swampy ground. Animals could have moved during the night. Within ten minutes Emma had found a small male anaconda, perhaps 1 m (3 ft) long. Two minutes later Jésus found a larger one, then nearby Renee found a humped shape in the mud that looked out of place. It was a large anaconda. We filmed my genuine excitement at the discovery, but now we had to catch her. We knew the snake was a female because of her size, as with all giant constrictors females are the larger sex, although anacondas take this dimorphism to an extraordinary degree. Males are just one fifth of a female's weight and about a quarter of their length. This is the biggest size discrepancy between the sexes of any vertebrate except fish. This is probably so they don't compete for the same sorts of food, and also to help females cope with the rigours of pregnancy.

During the breeding season females exude a chemical message or pheromone from between their scales which draws males towards them. Females of

Above, An aquatic snake, the green anaconda is found in the swamps and lakes of tropical South America and in Trinidad. Here an anaconda constricts a caiman – look at the girth of its coils

other species of boa or python, usually attract one or perhaps a few suitors; a female anaconda can have an entourage of up to 14. The ones we had caught that morning were probably on their way to or returning from the female I was about to catch.

Anacondas form into mating balls. At first the males check out the female with a frenzy of tongue flicking. If everything goes well, one or two of them will bring into play the vestigial limbs at either side of their vent; boas and pythons use these hard, sharp spurs to scratch and stroke the female. The successful male will then mate with the female. All male snakes have a pair of penises. Depending upon how his tail lies in relation to the female's, the male will insert either the left or the right one. If he gets the chance, once he has finished with one he'll then use the other, which increases his chances of successfully fertilising her. Pythons lay eggs, whereas anacondas are boas and bear live young, retaining their eggs within their bodies until hatching and then giving birth to a litter of babies. Anacondas have between 20 and 40, each one individually wrapped in it own egg membrane. They use a tiny egg tooth on their snouts to cut an exit in this transparent capsule. While they are gravid, female anacondas cannot afford the risk of being injured by their prey. This, and the fact that they have tighter skins because of carrying their young, gives less flexibility for expansion after meals which means they don't eat for seven months. Coping with this ordeal may be one of the reasons they have to grow so large.

The humped shape in the mud hadn't moved and there wasn't a scale to be seen. I had no idea of her actual size, so this was a form of lucky dip – or an unlucky dip if I missed her head and was bitten. I'd been bitten earlier by one of the small males and spots of blood had just stopped forming on the puncture wounds; a bite from a large female would not be life threatening, but it would be painful, and I didn't want to experience it.

I felt under the mud and the anaconda started to move forward. I glimpsed the head in a patch of clear water and lunged. My fingers gripped her neck and she thrashed her muscular body. I had grabbed some weed as well which made her slippery but I managed to hold on. Jésus and Renee gathered up the rest of her body. The realisation of my dream didn't disappoint. The anaconda was immensely strong just as I had expected, her muscular coils glistened in the sunlight. The top of her greenish body had large black blotches, while her undersurface was sulphur-yellow peppered with small dark spots, her face was gorgeous with orange and black stripes. Jésus found a mating plug in her vent, a package of hard proteinaceous material inserted by the male that had mated with her, to stop any other prospective suitors doing the same. Back at the field laboratory a sample of her blood would be taken. Jésus is building a genetic database for as many of the snakes in his study area as he can, and she would be measured and weighed. I guessed she was 6 m (20 ft) long and she weighed 97 kg (214 lb). I later found out she was 5.5 m (18 ft) long and I wondered how big the biggest anacondas really get.

The Llanos is probably not the place to find a giant; for part of the year it is dry and anacondas often have to move overland to find any pools that remain. All of the giant snakes show a predilection for habitats associated with water. Indian and African pythons show some preferences for mammal burrows or other refuges with nearby bodies of water, reticulated pythons are often near water courses or swampy ground – I had caught mine in a monsoon drain. The anaconda is of course the most aquatic of them all.

Water helps giant snakes maintain their body temperature. The temperature of water remains more constant than that of air: if the air temperature drops, snakes can immerse themselves to stay warm; if it becomes too high, they can use the water to lower their body temperature. Staying under a layer of water cloaks snakes from the eyes of predators and also provides concealment as they sit and wait to ambush their own prey. Most importantly for a discussion on how big anacondas may grow, water supports their great mass, making movements less demanding in terms of energy. Even the female I'd caught, although not fully grown, somehow felt less compact than other species of boas and pythons that I had held. This is because for most of the time her body is held firm by the pressure of the water.

That's why it's likely that if there are any really gigantic anacondas, long enough to claim the New York Zoological Society's fabled and steadily-increasing reward (the society first offered US$1,000 many years ago, and the reward now stands at US$50,000 for any live healthy snake 9.14 m (30 ft) or more in length), they will be found somewhere in the permanent rivers of the Amazon rain forest. If such an impressive giant were ever to be found, I for one, would certainly be at the front of the queue to see it.

Sharks

The formidable great white is probably the best-known shark species, immortalised by the film *Jaws*. It is not the world's biggest fish, however, and averages a mere 4.5 m (15 ft). This accolade belongs to the whale shark, and the largest on record was 12.2 m (40 ft 7 in) long. Only a small proportion of the world's 350 shark species are known to attack people and so their fearsome reputation is generally undeserved.

THE CORAL SAND AND TROPICAL VEGETATION THAT MARKS THE COAST OF NEW Providence Island in the Bahamas lay ahead of us. Above us, immense thunder clouds towered high into the sky. Lurid, fluorescent pink and luminous orange, they were illuminated by the tiniest sliver of a sunset. Colours as vibrant as these were a sign of an imminent storm. As I turned to slip my arms into my diver's back pack and take the weight of my air cylinder, the light was extinguished, darkness comes so quickly in the tropics. Our boat was a short distance away from the shore, lying between us and the island was a rolling, black, satin sea.

My companion and I felt a palpable tension; it wasn't just the weather that made everyone slightly nervous about what we were about to do. My mouth felt dry, a sensation that was exacerbated by my breathing equipment, which more closely resembled a welder's mask than a diver's one. The device covered my whole face; the air-filled void between my face, and the transparent front would allow me to speak underwater. As soon as I was submerged, a small microphone near my mouth and a radio link to the surface, ensured that every exclamation I made or nervous breath I took, could be heard by sound recordist Mark Roberts, who was high and dry in the boat. As a backup – underwater communications systems are notorious for malfunctioning – I also had a small tape machine on my back which would record me directly. I hoped that Mark couldn't hear the flutter of the butterflies in my stomach. This was my first ever night dive, and the first time I had dived with sharks in pitch

Above, A smaller relative of the Caribbean reef shark, the blacktip reef shark is found in the Pacific. Compared to its Caribbean counterpart that reaches 3 m (10 ft), the blacktip reef shark reaches only 1.8 m (6 ft). However, it is still a danger to humans

darkness. The Caribbean sea was warm enough for just shorts and a T-shirt, so I felt a greater freedom under the water than usual – wet suits tend to restrict movement. The crew followed, there was an eerie feeling, particularly as the storm had started in earnest. Every so often the scene would light up as if a battery of flash guns had been discharged. Cameraman Mike Pitts pushed his camera ahead of him, director Bill Butt was at his side; he carried futuristic metallic pods, the filming lights and Dave the dive leader carruied the bait, some chunks of fish. We settled ourselves on the reef 15 m (49 ft) below the surface, at the edge of a drop off, that plunged out of sight below us.

Bill tested the lights and I noticed how the chain mail on my left arm gleamed. Later I'd be relieved that I wore this gauntlet. Dave passed me a hand-sized fish head which I waved in the current. Minutes ticked by, then three Caribbean reef sharks arrived; this was the vanguard, soon we were surrounded. Supremely elegant, the sharks were illuminated by our powerful lights. Their sleek form was branded on to my retina by a lightning flash; snow white below and steel grey above. They moved with streamlined speed, those classic shark dorsal fins set far back down their bodies. This is a characteristic of requiem sharks, the family to which they belong.

Cautious at first, they soon began to come closer for the bait. I almost had to push the fish head into the mouth of the first one. Close up the smiling slit seemed to be more teeth than mouth. Mike filmed as one after another, the pieces of bait disappeared. At one stage there were sharks swimming between our legs; another bumped the camera and lights, and one shook my arm like a dog shaking a bone and I thought I'd be dragged over the drop off. Caribbean reef sharks can only exert about the same pressure with their jaws as we can with ours, so I wasn't bruised, but without the chain mail glove those teeth would have slashed my arm to pieces. The shark wasn't being malicious – to give Mike a longer shot I'd held onto a bait a fraction too long and the frustrated shark had worked its mouth around my arm in case that was the way to sever its meal. Reef sharks feed almost exclusively on fish. They wouldn't have been interested in chickens or rabbits and they certainly didn't consider us a potential meal.

When they materialised from the dark they seemed bigger than they were. Large females grow to just over 3 m (10 ft). Without anything to compare it to for scale it was difficult to judge their size. This was why I wanted to get into the water to show how my 1.9 m (6 ft 2 in) body compared with the sharks when we were swimming side by side. The ones I met in the Bahamas were the smallest we'd filmed, even though by the standards of most sharks they were large and stout. There are nearly 500 species of shark, 80 per cent of which are smaller than us. The average shark is 90–130 cm (3–4 ft 3 in) long at maturity, and feeds on small fish. The smallest of the small is the spined pygmy shark which is 15 cm (6 in) long when fully grown.

Whale Shark

To swim with the world's largest shark, I had to travel from England to north-west Australia, not once but twice during the month of April. From March to June, autumn in the southern hemisphere, whale sharks congregate on the ocean side of Ningaloo Reef, one of the world's longest fringing reefs. This intricate system of coral stretches over 260 km (79 miles) and, at some points, is only a short distance from the beach.

Unfortunately, April occurs at the tail end of the cyclone season in tropical Australia, and on my first visit to Exmouth, a small town about 1,270 km (387 miles) north of Perth, whale shark watching was on hold because of Cyclone Vance. Rated as a severe tropical storm category five, the most powerful you can get, it was tracking along the coast right towards the town. When meteorologists predicted that Vance was 12 hours away, Exmouth was put on red alert. Because of the danger everyone was asked to stay inside and we were grounded in our motel rooms. Everyone hoped the cyclone would spin out to sea but it didn't. We were right in its path, and Exmouth was devastated by the strongest winds ever to strike the Australian mainland, over 200 kph (124 mph). Miraculously nobody was killed, but boats were flipped from the harbour as if they were toys, hundreds of houses were flattened and vital services decimated. It would be some weeks before the chaos was over and normal activities resumed, so our only option was to return to England. It was a sobering thought. Our purpose in Exmouth was 'only television' and Cyclone Vance had given us an extra opportunity. We'd filmed an exciting sequence of me right in the middle of a giant weather system. This wasn't exactly what we had planned, but we had time to come back for the whale sharks. The cyclone wasn't so benevolent to the people that lived there. It had destroyed homes, possessions and even livelihoods. Three weeks later Exmouth still wasn't open for business so cameraman Gavin Thurston, sound recordist Jeremy Ashton and I, based ourselves at Coral Bay, a small community further south that had avoided a direct hit by Cyclone Vance.

Within three hours of arriving from England we were on a boat in the deep water at the edge of the reef. Above us a pilot in a spotter plane scrutinised the sea; whale sharks spend most of their time at the surface, so aerial surveys are the most efficient way of finding them. It didn't take long before the pilot had located one. It was south of our position, but with ship-to-air radio, he guided our craft towards the great fish. At sea level our first view was of the top of the tail, the huge, sabre-shaped caudal fin just breaking the surface. In all sharks the tail is the main propulsive organ. Whale sharks need a tail over 3 m (10 ft) long to propel their massive bulk throughout the ocean. As the whale shark came closer, from time to time the water dipped

Above, Cyclone Vance hit the town of Exmouth on our first visit to film whale sharks. It was rated as severe tropical storm category five

Right, Silhouetted against the surface of the sea the outline of the whale shark is unmistakable. The one I saw was a male with white claspers by its anal fin

to reveal the first and largest of its two dorsal fins (shark species have either one or two). These and the two sets of paired fins, the pectoral and pelvic fins (the former are located under the body in the front, the latter under the body in the middle), are also used for propulsion, but their main purpose is to fine-tune movements along all three axes as the shark moves through the water.

Compared to the fastest shark, the mako, which is capable of high-speed bursts of 56 kph (35 mph), the whale shark is relatively slow, swimming with deliberation at 5 kph (3 mph), but probably able to reach 16 kph (10 mph) if pushed. The cruising speed is easy for an Olympic swimmer, but I am certainly not in that class, and Olympic swimmers don't have to push heavy underwater cameras as Gavin had to. Unless this was a really amenable individual, we had to circle around, position ourselves in its path, jump in, and be ready to film before it was upon us.

Hanging in the water in my snorkel gear, I dipped my head below the surface to see the leviathan approaching. If you can imagine something the length and bulk of a single decker bus swimming straight at you, you're halfway to understanding how I felt. Whale sharks are by far the largest fish in the sea. It is claimed that one caught at Baba Island near Karachi, Pakistan in 1949 measured 20 m (65 ft) long, 7 m (23 ft) around the thickest part of its body, and weighed around 20 tonnes. Between 10 and 12 m (33–39 ft) is a more usual maximum size. The largest to be accurately measured

was a male caught in Bombay, India in 1983, and was 12.2 m (40 ft 7 in) long.

Our shark was about 6 m (20 ft) long and probably weighed 6 tonnes. It came straight at me, and I peered into its eyes which seemed tiny in comparison to the rest of its broad head. They lay just above the corners of the mouth, which was 1 m (3 ft) across and seemed to be smirking at me. I was grinning to myself: you can't help feeling euphoric during a close encounter such as this. The massive creature was nearly upon me, slowly the mouth opened, and I paddled furiously to get out of the way. Whale sharks are gentle giants but colliding with one isn't to be recommended. Compared to the reef shark this one was all mouth and no teeth. Whale sharks do have teeth, several thousands in all, arranged in about a dozen rows, but they're only 30 mm (1 in) long.

As it passed me five gill slits on the side of its head flared open. This was the exit point for the large volumes of water flowing into its mouth and over its gills. These have two functions. First they extract oxygen from sea water. Here the gas is much less concentrated than in air, about $\frac{1}{30}$ volume, so sharks need to take in a huge amount of water to breathe, particularly one as large as this. Secondly, the whale shark is one of three species, the other two being the basking shark and megamouth, that feed by filtering tiny planktonic organisms up to the size of small fish, from sea water. The gill openings of these sharks are lined by a series of comb-like gill rakers which act as a colander to strain plankton, most of it rice-sized, from the water. An abundance of food is probably what draws whale sharks to Ningaloo Reef. It was a sobering thought that in my excitement I must have swallowed mouthfuls of thin planktonic soup, not that this would have made any dent in the food supply.

The whale shark seemed oblivious to its film crew entourage and even slowed down so Gavin had time for shooting and I could be enthralled at a leisurely pace. We were temporary visitors to a whole community of swimmers. As well as us, the giant was accompanied by shoals of small fish; most were bright yellow, the young of golden trevally. They danced in shafts of sunlight, darting right into the shark's mouth whenever our shadows passed over them. The odd one or two could perhaps be swallowed but having cover from predators out in open water makes this a risk worth taking. At one point I was joined by one of the passengers. The sinuous fish, about the length of my forearm, gave me quite a start as it actually seemed to attach itself to my leg for a moment. It was a remora, a frequent hitchhiker with many of the larger sharks, which either has an easy ride by swimming in the larger fishes' wake, or an entirely free ride securing itself with a sucker on to the shark's body. In return remoras clean up the parasites that infest a shark's skin. To gain a real impression of the whale shark's overall beauty I had to hang back and give it some distance. Dark grey in colour, its skin was patterned with white lines and a mosaic of white polka dots, some of them so bright they seemed to shine with their own inner light. This dot and dash arrangement is as unique as a fingerprint and individual sharks can be identified by their markings. Sometimes the leviathan left the surface to swim at a depth of 3 m (10 ft). Snorkelling directly above I could look down on the broad back. Three pronounced ridges gave the creature the feel of being one of those amoured prehistoric fish. In fact the back is the toughest part of the body and if it can't swim away, turning its back on you is this creature's one and only defensive manoeuvre.

Catching up with the whale shark I dived down right underneath it. The huge white belly gleamed in the sun as rays bounced back up from the sea bed. I smiled and a few bubbles of air left my mouth. They frightened the flotilla of fish sheltering beneath the shark which scattered in all directions darting between and over the top of the pectoral fins which flared out from the front of the body. A pair of cylindrical white sausages

trailed out from either side of the anal fin at the base of the tail. These were the claspers, only male sharks have them, and they are used for implanting sperm inside the female during mating.

Little is known about reproduction in this species. Until a few years ago nobody was even sure whether they laid eggs or gave birth to living young. In 1953 an egg case larger than a football and containing a 36.8 cm (14.5 in) whale shark embryo was found in a trawl net in the Gulf of Mexico. The find started a controversy that went on for 42 years. Were whale sharks egg-layers or had this egg resulted from a premature birth? Did the females never lay their eggs, instead retaining them inside their bodies until the young had hatched, rather than giving birth to a litter of babies? The debate was ended in 1995 when a Taiwanese fisherman harpooned a 10.6 m (35 ft) pregnant whale shark which was examined by a team from the National Taiwan Ocean University. Three-hundred embryos, ranging in size from 40–63 cm (16–25 in) in length, were found inside the mother's body proving that whale sharks give birth to live young. Of the 300 embryos, 15 were still alive and ready to be born.

The male whale shark had honoured us with his company for three hours or more, usually interactions last for just a few minutes, so we'd been very lucky. This whale shark was so amenable that if we lagged behind, he hovered in the water, or slowed down as if he was waiting for us. We'd shot 30 minutes of film and I had certainly achieved my aim of using myself swimming next to the shark to give an idea of scale.

Whale sharks are found throughout the world in tropical and warm temperate seas. In deep waters the megamouth shark takes up their plankton-feeding role; in colder seas the basking shark does the same.

Below, A whale shark's eyes seem tiny in comparison to the rest of its broad head. Its huge mouth contains several thousand teeth, just 30 mm (1 in) long, arranged in about 12 rows

Megamouth and Basking Shark

The weird megamouth was first identified in 1976 and only 12 have ever been found worldwide. One was stranded on a beach in western Australia, another was caught in the Philippines, five have been sighted in Japan, two in California, another in Brazil and one in Senegal, west Africa. These fish have soft, flabby bodies. Their bulbous heads sporting enormous mouths give them a sinister appearance, but they are as timid as whale sharks. It is believed these deep water fish make vertical migrations to the surface at night, where their planktonic food flourishes. They may not be giants, the largest found so far was 5 m (16 ft 6 in) long, but nobody really knows how big they can get.

Encounters between people and basking sharks are much more frequent. The species often feeds at the surface during daylight hours; sailors thought they were basking in the sunshine, hence their name. Not as prettily marked as a whale shark, basking sharks are a uniform dark blue, brown, charcoal or grey on their underside. They are ranked second in size, and the biggest to be accurately measured became entangled in a herring net in the Bay of Fundy, Canada in 1851. It was 12.3 m (40 ft 6 in) long. A size of 15 m (49 ft 6 in) has also been claimed but not authenticated. In fact few exceed 10 m (33 ft); a heavyweight of this size weighs 3 tonnes or more. They make up for being the second largest shark by having a cavernous mouth, larger than a whale shark's, with very long, broad gill slits – the first pair almost meet below the throat. Oversized jaws agape, they swim for hours through thin and thick swarms of plankton. A large one filters 1,850 cu. m (65,371 cu. ft) or 2,000 tonnes of water every hour, which is the equivalent of an Olympic-sized swimming pool. Particles of food

are sieved out by the gill rakers. Water flows through this sieve-like structure, but any particles denser than water collide with the gill rakers and stick, a phenomenon known as inertial impaction. It is important that the gill rakers do not get clogged because after food has been filtered out, the water must continue to give up its oxygen to the respiratory action of the gills. In British waters the preferred food is small reddish copepods, shrimp-like creatures, which are around 5 mm (0.2 in) long; similar kinds of animals may be consumed in other parts of the world.

Much of the life of the basking shark remains mysterious. Several have been caught during the winter which had lost their gill rakers. Food is scarce during that time, and it is thought that they don't attempt to feed, and are unable to eat until their gill rakers grow back four to five months later. It is possible that they rest on the ocean floor surviving on food stored in their liver. No pregnant females have ever been observed, and the three smallest reported so far ranged in size from 1.7 m (5 ft 5 in) to 2.6 m (8 ft 6 in),

Left, Basking sharks are found all over the world in cool and temperate seas and oceans. They can reach up to 15 m (49 ft) but usually measure around 10 m (33 ft)

Below, While swimming the basking shark keeps its mouth open filtering swarms of plankton

so basking sharks probably measure 1.5–2 m (5–6.5 ft) at birth.

Adult specimens have a short, conical snout with a rounded tip. Smaller, younger sharks have a much longer snout, projecting far beyond the mouth, giving them a big-nosed appearance. In fact, young basking sharks were at first thought to represent a separate species. The snout gradually shortens to the adult shape, becoming more in proportion with the rest of the body, when the animals are 3.6–4.8 m (12–16 ft) long.

Basking sharks are sluggish and inoffensive. They do have thousands of teeth but these are minute and would be hopeless if used in an attack. These gentle giants are harmless to humans, just as whale sharks are, but as is often the case we do not respond in kind. They have been hunted mercilessly over the years, primarily for their livers. Unlike the majority of fish, sharks don't have a gas-filled bladder for buoyancy. Instead they have the ability to load their liver with oil to reduce their specific gravity. To help a basking shark float it has an enormous liver composed of up to 50 per cent squalene oil, a substance which is lighter than water. During the first half of the 18th Century, animal oils such as this were used for lighting purposes; a single basking shark could yield 364–1818 l (80–400 gallons) of squalene oil. Large numbers were taken in Massachusetts waters, especially off the tip of Cape Cod, to fuel the lamps of the colonists. Stocks were soon depleted as this fish is both slow to reproduce and slow-growing. Basking sharks are hunted on a smaller scale today in Norway, the Lofoten Islands, Portugal and California. The bodies can be used as a source of fish and animal feed. Unbelievably, these docile and placid creatures are even known to be slaughtered for causing an inconvenience. Along the coast of British Colombia they sometimes swim into valuable fishing gear which they can damage when trying to escape. The fishermen also consider that they compete with salmon and cod for plankton. Fortunately attitudes among the public at large towards these impressive giants are more tolerant, and they have even become a tourist attraction.

Basking sharks are found in most temperate seas and are the largest fish found in the waters around the British Isles. In May 1998 literally hundreds of them made an imposing sight off the Lizard Peninsula, southern Cornwall. A large plankton bloom was probably responsible for this spectacular occurrence. I find it delightful to think of these sea-going giants living just off the coast of holiday resorts both here and in North America. A cruise to see these magnificent animals followed by scones, strawberry jam, clotted cream and a pot of tea in a Cornish tea-room seems to me to be a perfect combination. Nowadays sightings are becoming rarer in the United Kingdom and it is thought that numbers of basking sharks are dwindling. Thankfully in 1999 they were given full protection in British territorial waters and populations will hopefully recover.

Sleeper Shark

Unlike the basking shark, sleeper sharks are carnivores not planktivores. I saw the first of these giants in a place much less accessible than Cornwall's inshore waters, and to see it I had to dive under the ice. My quest began with a helicopter flight over Greenland, the world's largest island (excluding Australia which is an island continent), which is two and half times the size of New Guinea, the next biggest. Belonging to Denmark, the island is 52 times the size of the mainland territory. Even so, Greenland straddles the Arctic Circle and is surrounded by freezing polar water, and it seemed a most unlikely place to find giant sharks.

The stories of the origin of the name Greenland are many and varied. My favourite is that the island was deliberately misnamed in the 10th Century by the outlaw Eric the Red, in an attempt to lure settlers from Iceland. As we approached, the view from the cockpit of the aircraft was both spectacular and hostile: towering peaks glowered over ice fields and glaciers – the centre of the country boasts the largest ice field in the northern hemisphere which is an astounding 2,500 km (1,550 miles) long and 100 km (62 miles) wide. Even though it was May, pack ice still clung tenaciously to the shore. We flew low along the intricate coastline where the picturesque fjords also owed their genesis to great tongues of ice scraping away at the rock. Our destination was Manitsoq, a community of brightly painted wooden houses nestling on steep slopes leading down to the harbour, a settlement which is home to 3,000 people.

The next morning, cameraman Rick Price, sound man Roger Long and I gathered around as Niels Krog, our Danish host, cast a line holding a putrid piece of seal meat into a hole he and his Greenlandic companion had cut in the ice. Neither the rod or the line looked very sturdy, but this is what they were going use to land a Greenland sleeper shark, a species that gets so large that one individual had the complete carcass of a reindeer inside its stomach.

I couldn't wait until this strange creation was dragged onto the ice so Rick and I, each attached to a safety line, dropped through the ice, which was already congealing in the hole, and into the water. I wasn't cold as I was wearing a dry suit, and, as the name suggests, in a dry suit you keep totally dry, and you can wear as many warm layers as will fit underneath. Away from the hole our silvered bubbles sped upwards shattering on the ceiling of the ice above as if they were breaking mirrors. I looked down the thin fishing line into the dark void below. Sleeper sharks are abundant in polar and cold temperature waters in both hemispheres, the north Atlantic and Arctic, the south Atlantic and Antarctic. They inhabit some of the coldest waters in the world. They are deep ocean fish living down to at least 1,200 m (4,000 ft). I hoped this one wasn't that far down or my air might run out before I saw it.

I looked over at Rick who was pointing the camera downwards. Just on the limits of visibility but coming closer there was a large dark shape. I wondered just how large it was. Niels claimed that sleeper sharks reach 8 m (26 ft), but the largest on record was 6.3 m (21 ft) long, and weighed 1,020 kg (2,250 lb), and this

Below, The Greenland sleeper shark is the only polar shark of the Atlantic and lives in deep water down to at least 1,200 m (4,000 ft). Sleeper sharks are abundant in polar and cold temperature waters in both hemispheres, the north Atlantic and Arctic, the south Atlantic and Antarctic

is still huge. These sharks are not renowned for resisting capture and this one was no exception. For Niels it must have been like hauling in a heavy sack of potatoes. We signalled to him when the shark was about 5 m (16 ft) from the hole; we'd decided to give it some slack so Rick could film me swimming alongside.

Travelling right next to the brown-skinned shark was an eerie experience, mainly because of its eyes. They were opaque and stared lifelessly at me. Each one had a green slimy object dangling from it, as if the shark was suffering from conjunctivitis. These

grotesque streamers, about 6 cm (3 in) long, were parasites. Greenland sleeper sharks usually have one in each eye. They are copepods, a type of crustacean, which attach themselves to the cornea with clawlike appendages. The anchoring process causes a scar, and more damage is done as the copepod's body scrapes back and forth across the cornea, as it feeds on the layer of cells at the surface. The creature seriously impairs the shark's eyesight, but as much of their time is spent in the darkness of the ocean depths this isn't a great loss, and shark may actually be helped by the

Above, The dry suit I was wearing kept out the cold as I swam alongside the Greenland shark. As the suit keeps you totally dry you can wear as many layers underneath as you can manage

Right, The 5 m (16 ft) sleeper shark that we found was certainly not the largest ever, and made no attempt to resist capture, but still it was no easy matter hauling it out of the water

parasitic copepods. As I watched I was mesmerised by the parasite streamer; it danced and jiggled in eddies and currents caused by the swimming sharks. Fish may be entranced in the same way and it has been speculated that the parasites may serve as a lure bringing prey within reach of the shark's jaws.

The mouth was full of rows of sharp, dagger-like teeth. It was hard to imagine how this sluggish creature could swallow, let alone catch, larger and livelier animals, but apparently it is a voracious and versatile predator. Fish of all kinds are important food items, including fast-swimming salmon. However, this shark also devours marine mammals. Seals are a common prey item, possibly taken alive, but sleeper sharks are renowned carrion feeders, gathering to feast in great numbers around whaling stations and at fish processing operations. In these situations they have been observed using convulsive body movements to saw off bite-sized pieces; parts of drowned horses and an entire reindeer carcass have been found in really large sleeper sharks; this type of food is probably found as carrion, washed into the sea from rivers.

Still attached to the fishing line the shark had

obligingly swum circuits under the ice hole giving Rick plenty of opportunity to film me and the fish together. Now we hauled it onto the ice. We wanted to remove the hook from its mouth and get it back into the water as quickly as possible. I followed it out and immediately shredded the skin on my hands by stroking it. Sharks have a covering of dermal denticles, plate-like scales, anchored in their skin. These vary in form, and in many free-swimming oceanic sharks, they are small with parallel ridges on their crown, a design which helps cut down drag, by smoothing the flow of water over the shark. In sea-bed dwellers like the Greenland sleeper, swimming efficiency isn't quite so important, so the denticles protrude more – as I found to my cost. They are as tough as thorns.

This particular shark looked distinctly as if it had been over-indulging in the pub – it had a protruding belly and a much rounder body than the other sharks I'd seen. A huge, oily liver, one third of the shark's weight, was responsible for the bulging paunch. Like the basking shark, this organ is charged with squalene to keep its owner naturally buoyant, with this Greenland sleepers can cruise effortlessly just above the sea bed. This fish really lived up to its name; other than languid movements with its dorsal fin and the odd ripple of movement across its rather small gill clefts, it was so phlegmatic it hardly seemed alive.

After I had been filmed with this strange creature, Rick Price jumped back through the ice hole to film the shark returning to the polar waters. Not all Greenland sleepers that are caught are released. As with the basking shark there was a whole industry based around this species. Each liver could provide up to three barrels or 392 l (105 gallons) of commercially valuable oil. In the middle of the 19th Century 2,000–3,000 Greenland sleeper sharks were taken every year. The catch had risen to an astronomical 32,000 sharks per annum in 1914, but after that it declined steeply, and today it is no longer of major importance. Small numbers have always been caught by the Inuit peoples, and the Greenland sleeper shark has a place of its own in their culture. In Greenland there was a taboo about cutting hair with an iron utensil, so instead the sharp lower dental bands of this shark are made into tools that do the job just as well! The flesh is toxic when fresh but can be eaten by both people and sled dogs if it is carefully washed or dried. The shark smells so strongly of ammonia that legend has it that long ago an old woman washed her hair with urine, and was drying it

with a cloth when a gust of wind took the cloth from her hand, and carried it out to sea. There it turned into a skalugsuak, the Greenland sleeper shark.

This species is a mystery to scientists. There is little information on its life history; age and size at maturity are unknown, and nobody has observed it hunting prey in the depths, even though it is among the world's largest sharks.

Another species of sleeper shark which may approach or even exceed the length and bulk of its Atlantic cousin, is the Pacific sleeper, found off Russia, California and other western America states and Japan. Its habits are similar to Greenland sleepers as it frequents polar waters all year round and lives in deep waters, 238–2,000 m (780–6,562 ft). It is reported to reach lengths of 7.6 m (25 ft) although its average length and weight are 3.65 m (12 ft) and 320–365 kg (700–800 lb). How this lethargic species catches lively animals is another mystery; inside the stomach of one 3.9 m (13 ft) female there was a 136 kg (300 lb) haul of rex and dover soles.

Below, The shark we caught had a protruding belly and a round body. The shark's huge liver, charged with oil to keep it buoyant, accounts for one third of the shark's weight. This allows the shark to cruise effortlessly just above the sea bed

Hammerhead Shark

Found in much warmer waters is a tropical shark that approaches the 6 m (20 ft) mark, that is just as outlandish as the two sleepers: the hammerhead. There are nine hammerhead species, all named after their T-shaped heads, and the great hammerhead is the biggest. Found throughout the world in tropical and warm temperate seas, one individual accurately measured was 5.6 m (18 ft 4 in) long, and weighed 454 kg (1,000 lb). This species is olive- or brownish-grey above, and paler below. The hammer-shaped head is straight along the front margin except for one indentation in the centre; the shark's eyes and nostrils are carried on the tips of the hammer.

There are many theories to explain this extraordinary structure. Perhaps the flattened head acts as a hydrofoil and enables the fish to turn more quickly. Maybe it is to do with keeping the eyes and nostrils far apart; widely-spaced eyes may mean hammerheads are able to judge distances more accurately, and the separation of the nostrils may allow a greater volume of water to be chemically sampled during swimming. Could the 'winged' head merely be a device for scaring away predators, or is it simply concerned with feeding? The great hammerhead eats all sorts of fish, including other sharks, bony fish and shellfish, but stingrays are a particular favourite. Ninety-six stingray barbs were once found embedded in the head of one of these sharks, and so the curious arrangement may be designed to keep the shark's eyes out of the way of the tail barbs of its prey, Nobody is really sure of the purpose of the flattened head. It could be any combination of the theories, or none of them. But when there are controversial issues in natural history like this one, the speculation is all part of the fun.

All hammerhead sharks give birth to well-formed young. After a gestation of eleven months, great hammerheads have a litter of 6–42 babies. Remarkably the embryos are nourished in a comparable way to mammals. Nutrients and oxygen are passed from mother to young through structures similar to placenta and umbilical cords, and waste products are exchanged in the opposite direction. The placenta forms a couple of months after development has begun. The embryos start off within eggs and are sustained by yolk. When this is exhausted the empty yolk sac fuses with the uterus wall to form the placenta. Hammerheads also provide nutrients for the growing young from secretions into the uterus. Numerous hair-like projections called appendiculae stick out from the umbilical cord; these absorb the nourishment and pass it onto the embryo. To help make the birth more comfortable for the young sharks as well as their mother, hammerheads are born in a delightful way, with the 'wings' of their head folded back like ear muffs.

Other hammerhead species are the winghead shark which is found in the northern Indian Ocean and

Above, There are many theories to explain the extraordinary structure of the hammer-shaped head such as enabling depth perception, hyrodynamics and respiration, but nobody knows for sure

Northern Australia. This species is small (1.5 m, 5 ft) and harmless to humans. The scalloped hammerhead is larger, up to 4.2 m (14 ft), and is found in tropical waters throughout the world. It is possible that this species is dangerous to humans but it may be confused with the smooth hammerhead which is known to attack people. The bonnethead is another small hammerhead which is abundant in muddy inshore areas in the western Atlantic and eastern Pacific. It may occur in large schools and exhibits complex social behaviour. The smooth hammerhead also occurs in large schools and migrates to warmer waters in the winter. It is the most tolerant of temperate seas of all hammerhead species. It is known to display aggressive behaviour towards humans but there have been few reported attacks. It usually eats fish, including other sharks, shellfish and species that live on the sea floor.

Most hammerhead species are harmless to people. The great hammerhead may be an exception, and there are unofficial reports of humans being attacked, usually when spear fishing. There is no doubt that in certain circumstances the two giants amongst flesh-eating sharks, the tiger and the great white, can be dangerous to humans.

Above, Found in tropical waters the hammerhead shark approaches the 6 m (20 ft) mark. Named after their T-shaped heads there are nine hammerhead species in total; the largest is the great hammerhead which can reach up to 6.1 m (20 ft)

Tiger Shark

The tiger is the largest member of the requiem sharks. The group contains about 50 species which includes the Caribbean reef shark I had fed in the Bahamas, as well as blacktip, whitetip, lemon and blue shark. Named because of the black or dark grey vertical stripes that extend down the sides of its greenish-grey body (the stripes fade with age), the awe-inspiring tiger grows huge. The largest verified specimen caught in 1922 in the Gulf of Panama was 6.23 m (20 ft 9 in) and weighed 792 kg (1,760 lb). This species has a world-wide distribution in the tropics and is a warm weather visitor to more temperate seas. They are frequent on the east coast of the United States – a 4 m (13 ft), 807 kg (1,780 lb) shark was caught off a pier in North Carolina – and they have even been found in the English Channel, and one has also been recorded in eastern Iceland.

The tiger shark has a litter of 10–82 pups after a gestation period of 12–13 months. There is no placental connection with the mother as in the hammerheads; the eggs are merely retained in the female's body and never laid. The young hatch inside the female's body and it is at this point that she gives birth. This species usually stays inshore. Believed to be a nocturnal hunter it quarters coral and rocky reefs at night, dropping beyond the reef edge to 150 m (500 ft) in the day. These activity patterns are far from predictable though; in the Leeward Islands they'll gulp down fledgling albatross chicks day and night if given the chance, and they've also been seen in pursuit of sting rays in shallow water.

The teeth of sharks are like disposable razor blades; there are a number of rows along the margins of the jaws. The first row is at the rim of the mouth. Lines of replacement teeth are forming all the time, and these move forward in a conveyor belt-like fashion, so the front line of blunt or broken teeth fall out and the line behind moves in to take up their position. In each jaw tiger sharks have 18–20 rows of distinctive teeth. They are asymmetrical, angular, finely-serrated and sharp; the triangular pointed rows point obliquely outwards. With these it can eat virtually anything, preferably with at least a component of animal protein. Three overcoats, a driver's license, one cow's hoof, the antlers of a deer, 12 undigested lobsters and a chicken complete with feathers and bones was the haul from one giant. In 1948, a tiger shark from west Africa was found to contain a tribal drum, 27 cm (10.75 in) in height, 25 cm (9.75 in) wide, weighing 6 kg (13.5 lb); the inside of the shark's stomach had been grazed by the drum's sharp edges. Actual prey items include turtles, fish, seals and birds. Basically a hungry tiger shark will swallow anything it comes across. This together with their size makes them particularly dangerous and they have been implicated in more fatal attacks on people than any other species. This isn't because they are an enemy of humans, but simply because they have big appetites.

Right, The tiger shark has 18–20 rows of finely-serrated, razor-sharp teeth in each jaw. As a result the shark is able to eat virtually anything

Great White Shark

In most people's minds, all sharks and particularly 'man eaters', are symbolised by the largest carnivorous species, the great white. It is one of two giants in the sea that prefer warm-blooded prey, the other being the killer whale. Our impressions of this creature are usually based on myths and legends and films such as *Jaws* than the sharks themselves.

Their size is certainly exaggerated. When fully grown their average length is 4.3–4.6 m (14–15 ft) with a weight of 322–770 kg (1,150–1,700 lb). However, there have been many fisherman's tales of their size; the biggest that has been properly verified was caught by Alfred Cutajar off the coast of Malta in 1987. It was 7.6 m (23 ft) long. The monster in *Jaws* measured 7.6 m (25 ft). This fictional beast, longer than any white shark known in nature, was in fact a composite of three model sharks – one shot from the left, one shot from the right and one shot 'in the round' – melded with footage of real great whites filmed off Dangerous Reef in Southern Australia. The model shark was much longer than these live ones, so for a scene where ichthyologist Matt Hooper (played by Richard Dreyfus) comes face-to-face with the killer while protected by a shark cage, a half-sized cage and a midget stunt man were used. This had the effect of making the 3.6–4.3 m (12–14 ft) shark, the size usually found in South Australian waters, look gigantic.

The white shark's notoriety as a blood-thirsty predator with a taste for human flesh is also undeserved. World-wide there have been only 245 documented attacks since 1876 and of these only 60 or so were fatal. To put this into perspective, since 1979 in the United States over 300 people have been killed by domestic dogs.

During the filming for *Giants* I hoped to get to grips with the real white shark but first we had to find one. The species is probably the widest ranging living shark, found in cold water in high latitudes, and temperate as well as tropical seas. However, it is becoming increasingly rare, probably because of us – great whites are killed incidentally by fishermen and deliberately by hunters.

Our quest began in Port Lincoln, a short flight from Adelaide in South Australia. The crew and I boarded the prawn trawler, *Miss Riley*. We were joined by Australian shark experts, Rodney Fox and his son Andrew, two of the world's foremost authorities on the natural behaviour of white pointers. (The Australian name for great white refers to the way in the which the front of the shark's head tapers to a cone.) Rodney should certainly bear a grudge against these huge fish – he has the scars to prove it. He was attacked in 1963, and since then he has shown the massive pale scar that circles his torso hundreds of times. Even though he has recounted the story for film crews many times, his tale is so compelling that we had to film him telling it once again.

He was taking part in a spear fishing competition 88 km (55 miles) south of Adelaide when he found himself in the mouth of the white shark. Scrabbling to gouge at its vulnerable eyes he must have struck a sensitive area as for some reason the shark let go and he floated up to the surface. Relief was brief as the shark came at him again and this time the two of them became linked by the fish line that hung from Rodney's waist. Dragged down and down he thought he would drown but suddenly the line snapped or was bitten through and he shot to the surface once more. This time a boat was at hand, and badly injured, he was helped on board and rushed to the shore. To survive this near-fatal attack, he now had incredible luck. An ambulance happened to be on the beach and it rushed him to Royal Adelaide Hospital in less than an hour. Miraculously there was a surgeon on duty who had just returned from England from a specialised course in chest surgery. Rodney was

Above, The reputation of the great white tends to give the impression that it is a monstrous shark. The truth however is more modest and the shark is not the ruthless human predator it is portrayed as. When fully grown their average length is 4.3–4.6 m (14–15 ft) and they weigh 322–770 kg (1,150–1,700 lb)

Far right, Immortalised by Hollywood the dorsal fin of the great white strikes fear into swimmers throughout the world

only held together by his wet suit and it took 426 stitches to sew him back together again. He doesn't bear a grudge because he recognises that being in waters patrolled by white sharks and surrounding yourself with straggling, bleeding fish that you've speared certainly increases the chance of an attack.

Our first destination was Hopkins Island, a place made enchanting by the antics of its resident sea lions. Like a pack of dogs running to greet a beloved owner they galloped down the beach towards our landing party. This was an opportunity to see the size of the prey that adult white sharks can attack. Rick Price, the cameraman, filmed the sea lions playing with me underwater. The females were about 2 m (6 ft), 90 kg (198 lb) – about the same as me. The bull seemed immense – three times my size – and it really brought it home that only a mega-carnivore could incapacitate

Above, This huge colony of fur seals breeds on the Neptune Islands in South Australia and inevitably attracts great whites. Nearby Dangerous Reef was where the footage of real sharks was shot for the film *Jaws*

Below right, We set off by boat from the small town of Gainsbaai, south-east of Cape Town in our bid finally to find a great white shark. Our target lay 45 minutes ahead of us out to sea

one of these creatures. To carry out this feat a white shark will usually make a vertical lunge, rushing upwards from a depth of 5–10 m (16–33 ft) to deliver a massive bite. The sea lion and shark could be carried about 1 m (3 ft) into the air by the force of the charge. The success of the hunt is dependent on the extremely destructive nature of the attack – the prey must be injured sufficiently by the initial impact that it is unable to retaliate. Once the initial attack is over, the shark hangs back and waits for up to five minutes until the prey is weakened by loss of blood, before delivering the final coup de grace.

Only a really large, hungry white shark would risk an attack on a bull sea lion – the mammal's sharp claws and teeth can cause serious injury. The shark's eyes are particularly vulnerable even though they take the precaution of rolling them in their sockets before biting to keep them away from sharp, dangerous objects. This is why white sharks will wait before following up an initial attack and why they prefer smaller, weaker pups to strong, healthy adults. Smaller white sharks have a different diet to the larger ones, they prey mainly on fish and to this end they even have teeth that are long and narrow for grasping slippery, scaly food. Adults have huge, broad serrated teeth for tearing off chunks of flesh or cutting through tough hides. They do not feed exclusively on pinniped colonies, however, and their catholic tastes include other sharks, squid, penguins, dolphins and whales. Sharks have a special penchant for the carcasses of whales. In fact scientists theorise that whale meat keeps large whites alive when sea lions are out of

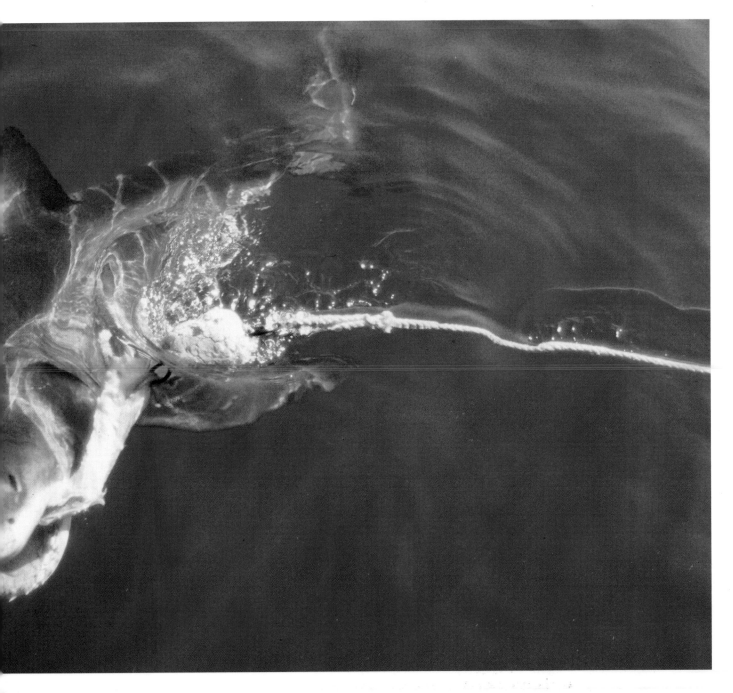

Above, After less than 20 minutes we saw our first shark! Anchors at the back and front of the boat held us in position as we filmed the shark from the deck. After our efforts in Australia we could hardly contain our excitement

season. By now you must be thinking that I was being foolhardy swimming with Australian sea lions, a preferred prey item, within the range of great whites, but Rodney assured me that the predators didn't cruise this particular bay.

The nearby Neptune islands were an entirely different proposition, home to a sprawling breeding colony of fur seals that definitely attracted sharks. Only a few years before a fisherman had been attacked and killed by a white shark. We set anchor just offshore

and began 'burleying' – releasing a steady stream of fish blood into the ocean from a huge container. The slick stretched out behind us and hopefully white sharks would be lured along this smelly route right to us. A few longer, larger fish chunks tied to ropes marked with coloured ballons floated closer in. If the baits had bites taken out of them or if the balloons disappeared below the surface we would know there was a shark in the vicinity. Two shiny aluminium cages were ready at the stern. Now all we could do was wait and wait and our vigil continued day after day. We changed locations once or twice, chugging from the flat, rocky islets of the North Neptunes to the flat rocky islets of the South Neptunes, finally trying the water of Dangerous Reef which had proved a reliable location in the past. Over seven days we must have put hundreds of gallons of fish and oil into the sea but the scent trail brought in nothing as far as we could see there wasn't a sniff of or by a white shark.

'No shows' like this one have happened more frequently in recent years. Great whites are protected in Australian waters but their population may have started to dwindle before this legislation came into operation. There are no hard statistics but it appears that people are sighting fewer of them. Slow to grow and reproduce, it may be that trophy hunters have exterminated most of the animals old enough to breed. When they do breed, white sharks give birth to a litter of fully-developed young, a baby is about 1.5 m (5 ft) long. Hopefully the South Australian population will be replaced when this new generation of protected sharks begin to reproduce. Unfortunately the crew and I couldn't wait that long and my quest continued on the watery margins of another fur seal colony, this time at the tip of South Africa.

The small town of Gainsbaai, south-east of Cape Town was our base. From the town's jetty it was only 45 minutes by boat to the flat rock of Dyer Island which seethed with thousands of South African fur seals. With anchors at the back and front of the boat we could contain the swell, wind and current and hold a position of sorts, although the craft still rocked, bucked and rolled. Brian the skipper soon had a slick of fish oil and baited lines in the water in much the same way as in Australia. He also had a secret weapon for attracting white sharks – Gladys, a flat polystyrene cut-out in the shape of a seal. A hunting shark aroused by the odour of food in the water around us, would see the silhouette at the surface, and approach to investigate. She certainly seemed to do the trick and after many fruitless days in Australian waters I was jubilant when in just 20 minutes a white shark nuzzled the cut-out. Brian hauled Gladys closer, drawing the shark towards our baits. At last I'd set eyes on the most famous dorsal fin in the world and there was much more to come. I was with the crew that had missed sharks in Australia and they were as excited as I was. Two cine cameras were whirring as the 4 m (13 ft) shark cautiously butted the fish. The film that Mark Yates was about to shoot would reveal the action of a bite slowed down by 20 times. Cameraman Rick Price was on deck with another camera to film this first encounter from a different angle. Water cascaded from the great conical snout as the shark lifted its head clear of the water, slowly it submerged and then lunged for the bait. In a cloud of spray and foam it bit down on the long strip of tough

Below, I watched the shark as it bit down on the bait. The elegant movement is facilitated by the loose connection between the upper and lower jaws which provide extreme mobility. The power of the great white's bite is phenomenal – as we know arms and legs can be removed with a single snap of these terrifying jaws

material. Skillfully hauling in the line Brian played the shark so we could see the jaws in action.

I could see the shark's eyes roll in their sockets as it bit down, but I could only appreciate the mechanics of a bite when we viewed the slowed-down action on film back in England. The bite was elegant in its simplicity. Both the upper and lower jaws are loosely suspended under the skull, and to give extreme mobility, they are only connected to the lower and outer rear corners. Watching the film you can see how the upper jaws laden with triangular teeth are moved downwards and simultaneously thrust forward protruding below the pointed snout, remarkably the over bite overlaps the lower jaw. Brutally efficient, the biting strength of a big shark is 3 tonnes per sq. cm (6.5 tons per sq. in), that's 60 kg (132 lb) on a single tooth. This power combined with the razor-blade dentition, means a white shark can tear off hunks of flesh from prey too large to swallow whole, or if it wanted to, hew off an arm or a leg.

The shots were spectacular, but all good things must come to an end, and in this case it was caused by a cascade of sea water onto the lens. Watching a screen filled with out of focus water took me right back to that rocking boat in Southern Australia. The shark had touched the side of the boat and was startled. It thrashed around trying to disengage its teeth making us and the equipment soaking wet. It flipped right over on its back before it achieved its aim, its snow white belly flashing in the sun, the feature that gives this shark its name.

As I was now wet through, it seemed as good a time as any to enter the shark's world and watch them from the cage under the water. Being careful not to tangle my scuba gear in the metal struts, I clambered in through the top of the cage. On the inside I was so heavily weighted I could stand right on the cage bottom, the line that held the cage to the boat was played out so it floated about 5 m (16 ft) away. Rick Price held his underwater camera at the back of the boat so we could film a shark in the watery void between the camera and the cage.

Unfortunately, the water was too murky to see the great fish in detail. Two sharks cruised around us however, and I could just make out their perfect hydro-dynamic shape. The two dorsal fins on the back, the front one being the largest – a graceful triangular sail – and below thre was a small diamond-shaped fin in front of the tail. Nearer the head, flaring out like wings,

the pectoral fins seem to provide a lift, as well as being used as brakes. Everything worked in unison so I felt I was watching something as efficient as a nuclear submarine or jet fighter. The giant tail swept from side-to-side effortlessly propelling the sharks through the water. Sometimes as if they noticed me, the sharks would flex their pectoral fins, stopping to hover in the water. Coming to any sort of halt is a rare event for great whites. As soon as they are born, they swim virtually continuously, relying on forward momentum to ram water through their open mouths and past their gills to breathe. However, this isn't true of all sharks. Some pump water past their gills when stationary by using muscles in their head and throat.

Following our first encounter conditions weren't right for the next nine days. We needed calm seas with a visibility of 8 m (26 ft) to try something very special. We decided to cut our losses and return a month later. When we returned a storm had passed through a few days before, but the strong current had swept floating particles kicked up by the storm away. As usual there was a swell but you could see through the water for at least 10 m (33 ft).

We had teamed up with Andre Hartman, a South African spear fishing champion. He and an American biologist Mark Marks had discovered that far from being lethal automotons, white sharks are choosy about what they bite, and in most circumstances are frightened of people. They'd found this out, tentatively at first, by swimming freely with the great fish.

As a 5 m (16 ft) shark circled the boat, we slipped into the water, with Rick Price the cameraman following closely behind. Andre urged us not to make

Above, Here you can see the way that the great white's hydrodynamic shape allows it to power through the water. There are two dorsal fins on the back, one large and one small, and two large pectoral fins on the underside of the body. The tail is crescent-shaped

any sudden movements. If this was a shy shark it would forgo any chance of a meal if he saw strange apparitions approaching and swim away. Nervously I put my head below the water, the adrenaline rush made me gasp a huge breath of air through my snorkel tube.

I was just 10 m (33 ft) away from the head of a great white shark with its characteristic clown's smile. It opened its mouth on the bait but didn't bite it. Perhaps the bait didn't feel quite right. Without tentacles, arms or fingers, the mouth and teeth of sharks are the main method a shark interacts with its environment. Alternatively we may have startled it. Whatever the reason, the shark lost interest in the food and swam straight at us – I was mesmerised. Head on, the girth of the shark's body seemed immense. As is the case with most giant creatures a small increase in length brings

on a disproportionate hike in bulk. The 4 m (13 ft) sharks I had seen from the cage were positively slimline in comparison to this.

The animal had white markings on its snout as if a child had scribbled on it with chalk. These were probably healed scars from battles with fur seals. There were no claspers dangling near the anal fin so this was a female. Passing languidly between Andre and myself, I felt she was gazing at me, and as I stared into that black eye I tried to imagine what it would feel like to be her. Trying was all I could do however, because in the shark's world even with scuba gear my land senses don't work too well, and today I was only snorkelling. Unless underwater technology radically changes, divers will always be half blind and deaf, coping with the twin problems of buoyancy and artificial breathing.

Below, The great white is probably the widest ranging living shark, found in cold water in high latitudes, and temperate as well as tropical seas, although it is less common in the latter. It is found mainly in coastal areas between the surface and depths of up to 1,280 m (4,200 ft)

Sharks, or something like them, have been around for some 300 million years and they have become highly evolved. Their basic design has changed little in that time however as it proved so successful from the start. With supreme hydrodynamic efficiency the shark we were watching hardly seemed to move as she circled us. She was already cruising faster than I can swim, and if she felt so inclined, she could be upon me with a burst of speed of over 15 kph (9 mph) even before I could spin round. She was also scrutinising me with a dazzling array of sensory systems of extraordinary sensitivity. Her eyes are similar to my own cornea, pupil, lens and retina but an abundance of cone receptors heightens the contrast between dark and light. My shape was silhouetted against the surface, and in this visibility she could easily perceive I wasn't a preferred prey item. She would also be able to tell this by smell; I hoped I didn't smell of seals or exude the scent of carrion, as precision chemical sensors in her nose can detect minute fractions of either. With these she may even be able to read the chemical components of the ocean itself, using concentrations of ordinary sea salts for navigation.

I didn't dare move as she came closer still. A shaft of sunlight danced over her head illuminating what seemed like five o'clock shadow around her mouth and chin. This wasn't stubble however; the scattered black dots are the pores of the ampullae of Lorenzini, which form another sensory system. They are named after an Italian anatomist, who first described them in 1878, although he didn't know their exact function. In fact the structures give sharks the ability to detect electrical fields that is unsurpassed. The pores open out into jelly-filled canals infiltrated by nerves which detect any electricity. Tests with some sharks show they can detect electrical fields equivalent to 0.01 microvolts per cm (0.394 in), which is the equivalent field produced by a AA battery with its terminals almost 1.6 km (1 mile) apart. The white shark would be sensing my beating heart and the impulses flashing through my muscles when I made any movement at all. She would also be reading the weak electric fields transmitted into sea water by the metal in the boat's outboard motor. This is probably the reason curious sharks will sometimes tentatively bite the metal of engines or cages.

The white shark was now broadside on, and I could see a line of larger pores running along her body, branching into a tracery around her face, another important sensory system, the lateral line. Anything from pressure waves from her own swimming bouncing back from objects in her path, or perturbations caused by the movements of prey, or my arms sculling to maintain position, would displace sensory cells inside jelly-filled tubes and send a message to her brain.

One of her senses I really didn't want her to test out on me, although it would probably save my life, was her soft tissue- and tension-sensitive jaws and teeth. More often than not, when they attack humans, white sharks back off and this is one of the reasons fatalities are rare. The tensile resistance they feel with the jaws tells them the prey they are attacking is not an animal covered in blubber. Humans have too much muscle and not enough fat to make hunting us worthwhile: large sharks would rather conserve their energy for predating marine mammals. Of course, attacks do happen, but they usually occur in murky water, with a hungry shark reacting to the possibility of a meal by wading in jaws first before sensing that continuing the attack would bring little reward. If white sharks lived up to their reputation, without any defence we should be sliced into pieces every time we encountered them. They certainly have the weaponry to make all attacks on us fatal, but they don't.

My shark dived below us, about 4 m (13 ft); we finned after her and from under the water Andre turned and smiled encouraging me to follow. I wasn't a spear fishing champion with the ability to hold my breath for a long time but I inhaled deeply and swam down after him. I can't describe the exhilaration of swimming right next to the majestic shark. Just before I ran out of breath I approached too closely and she shied away. My last view was of that great tail sweeping sideways propelling her beyond the limits of visibility.

Of course in the white shark's world human swimmers can never be 100 per cent safe, but perhaps we shouldn't expect the ocean to be a giant swimming pool where we can just swim into other creatures' territory. Sharks are a symbol of an untamed world of which we know tantalisingly little: their lives, how they are born, how long they live and where they go to die, are all still mysteries. Recent work has shown that they may associate with one another and form social groups. We love megacarnivores as long as they are extinct, but those that live among us are demonised and hunted to extinction. I hope this doesn't happen to the great white as there is still so much to find out about them.

Bears

The big three bears are the American black bear, the brown bear and the polar bear. The latter two vie for the title of the largest species: polar bears weigh an average of 500–600 kg (1,100–1,300 lb) while brown bears usually weigh around 780 kg (1,700 lb). When upright the polar bear can reach 3 m (10 ft) above the ground.

THESE GIANTS ARE SOME OF THE MOST POWERFUL ANIMALS ON EARTH. THERE are three species that grow to a great size and even the smallest of these will break down 9 m- (29.5 ft-) high oak trees, to get at the acorns at the top, bite through live trees thicker than a man's arm, or break into cars, ripping and twisting steel as if it was tin foil.

The second largest is even stronger and a suit has been developed for protection against being attacked by it. To test whether it would stand up to a giant's onslaught, the suit and its designer Troy Hurtubise did some field tests, which included colliding 18 times with a three-tonne truck at 50 kph (21 mph), being battered with a tree trunk weighing 136 kg (300 lb), withstanding shots from a 12-bore shot gun and an attack by bikers armed with axes and baseball bats. The biggest of the trio is no pushover either; it can flip a beluga, a small species of whale, from the sea with one swipe of its paw. All three can be a danger to humans. In fact, in North America they are responsible for far more deaths than rattlesnakes, but despite this, they're always in the top ten on lists of popular animals – of course I'm writing about bears.

Their popularity is probably due to their similarity to humans. They walk on the soles of their feet, not on their toes like dogs or cats. They can also pick things up with their paws and their eyes are in the front of their heads just as ours are. Bears have also been revered because of an important aspect of their behaviour. They disappear into their dens at the beginning of winter, miraculously emerging again when the snow begins to melt, sometimes with new-born cubs in tow. To some cultures this made them symbols of resurrection and virgin birth.

Bears also command our attention because of their size. There are eight species in the world; the smallest is about the size of a person, the largest the size of five people. If you take bulk into consideration, the discrepancy is even greater. The biggest bear weighs ten times as much as the smallest. The Malayan sun bear is at the diminutive end of the scale. It is found in dense forest throughout south-east Asia, where it feeds on insects and their larvae, and vegetables – particularly the growing tips of the coconut palm – and

spices up this diet with the odd bird, rodent or some honey. All bears love this sticky, sweet substance and sun bears are reported to show their intelligence when procuring it. A captive animal watched how a pot of honey was locked away in a cupboard. Later it opened the cupboard by turning the key with its claw.

The next largest bear, the giant panda, is probably one of the most familiar and yet the most enigmatic animal in the world. Until recently there was a question mark over whether it was a bear at all, and in the past century there have been over 50 scientific treatises discussing the question of how the giant panda should be classified. Was it an unusual kind of bear or a specialised racoon? Or does its uniqueness mean it should be in a carnivore family all of its own? Recent advances in molecular biology allowed the puzzle to be solved. Analysis of the panda's genetic material made it clear that the panda should be classified with the bears. The giant panda needs little

Below, Found high in the mountains of China, giant pandas feed for up to 12 hours a day, usually in that characteristic sitting position, and will consume as much as 12.5 kg (28 lb) of bamboo shoots and roots

to about double.

The mountainous regions of western Venezuela, Colombia, Ecuador, Peru and western Bolivia, are home to the spectacled bear. Its body is brown or black, but it gets its name from the striking creamy-white circles or semi-circles around its eyes. There is also a variable pattern of white on its neck, usually in the form of a half-moon, with lines extending down its chest. This bear roams the cloud forest in search of fruiting trees. If there's a good crop, it may even break branches to make a platform to feed from. When ripe fruits are hard to come by it still gets most of its food from the trees, tearing apart bromeliads to get at their succulent centres, ripping up young palms for new leaves that haven't yet unfurled, or stripping off tree bark to get at the sappy wood below. All bears are opportunists and the spectacled bear also eats the occasional mouse, bird or insect.

The similar-sized sloth bear of the Indian sub-continent has a very different feeding strategy. It has a coat of shaggy black fur with a white or yellow mark on its chest, in the shape of a 'Y' or a 'U', and has a long mobile white snout which gives a clue to what it preys upon – aardvarks and anteaters have a similar arrangement. Sloth bears break open the termite-mounds with their claws, then like other termite eaters, stick their snouts inside as far as they will go. They blow away any dirt and protrude their naked lips to make a funnel to hoover up termites, which are sucked through a gap in the front teeth. To avoid inhaling angry termites they can close their nostrils at will. The slurping noises that result can be heard nearly 200 m (610 ft) away. Even though the sloth bear has special adaptations for a diet of insects, it will also consume honey, eggs, carrion, grass, flowers and fruit.

The Asiatic black bear is a medium-sized bear that nearly makes the top three largest bears. Although the biggest males can have a body length up to 1.8 m (6 ft), the same as the American black bear, they are a much slighter animal with a maximum weight of 150 kg (330 lb) compared to the American black's 270 kg (595 lb). The western boundary of distribution is south-east Iran with Japan at the eastern limit. Another forest bear, it is an expert climber, especially when there are fruits and bees' nests to be had. None of the smaller bears mentioned so far hibernate but in the colder parts of its range, such as Siberia, the Asiatic black bear sleeps in a hollow tree or cave from November to March or April.

Above, Found on the Indian sub-continent sloth bears have a coat of shaggy black fur with a white or yellow mark on their chest, in the shape of a 'Y' or a 'U', and a long mobile white snout which is used to find termites

description. It is white over much of its body, but its limbs, ears and a band across its shoulders are black, and of course, its most endearing feature are the black patches over its eyes.

London Zoo's Chi Chi was in the news when I was six years old. She was flown to Russia for an amorous liaison with An An, the star of Moscow's zoo, but they didn't get on. Even though the blind date failed, her return was a great occasion, and I remember going to see her after she had been home for a week. She was sitting down as only pandas can, using her great stomach as a table for a pile of bamboo leaves, which she chewed through methodically. She manipulated the leaves with great dexterity, using her so called 'thumb', which is really the enlarged wrist bone. A Cub Scout group from Cornwall had the honour of providing Chi Chi's leaves every week – apparently bamboo grows well in the mild climate of south-west England. Even so, such large quantities of leaves were needed that her diet was bulked up with boiled chicken and rice.

High in the mountains of China, wild pandas rely on dense stands of bamboo for 99 per cent of their food. They spend up to 12 hours a day usually in that characteristic sitting position, consuming as much as 12.5 kg (28 lb) of bamboo shoots and roots. They need to eat a large amount because even though they are adept at choosing the most nourishing parts, bamboo is not a very nutritious food.

Spectacled and sloth bears are the next size up, although the former has a slightly bigger build. Male spectacled bears weigh 100–155 kg (220–342 lb) compared to 80–140 kg (176–309 lb) for a male sloth bear. In all species of bear, the males are heavier than the females; this size difference ranges from marginal

Black Bear

The third largest bear is also the most numerous. Called the American black bear, as its name suggests, it is found exclusively in North America. It is widely distributed and can be seen prowling along salmon streams in Alaska, lumbering through the canyons in Arizona, pushing through the laurel thickets of the Great Smoky Mountains, or sloshing through the mud in Florida's Everglades. These bears are found in at least 23 states in America and in every state in Canada. The American black bear has adjusted well to the development of North America and populations have remained remarkably constant.

I saw this species for the first time at one of the most extraordinary places I've ever visited, the Vince Shute Sanctuary, near Orr, Minnesota. The man this magical place is named after is in his eighties and still a regular visitor. In the 1950s if he received a visit from black bears he would shoot to kill, but he soon began to have regrets about this waste of life and wondered if it would be possible to live in harmony with the bears. He began by leaving them food in a meadow close to his cabin. By doing this and keeping his own food out of the way of their sensitive noses, they became placid neighbours, rarely trying to break into his cabin, as they once used to. Remarkably, the bears came to learn that people would never harm them in Vince's meadow. In summer, particularly late summer, when they were fattening up for hibernation, more and more bears arrived. Mothers would bring their cubs, and there would be newly weaned yearlings and huge adult males. These totally wild bears showed no aggression to people, though just outside the sanctuary they could be shot in the hunting season for trophies. Vince could stand right next to them, and this is still the case today. Bill and Klarie Lea have taken over the running of the sanctuary and as my guides, would show me these remarkable animals.

The first time I went out into the meadow I had to

ask if a stranger would be in any danger. Bill said that the bears sometimes charged to put the 'frighteners' on – lunging straight at you, slamming their front feet into the ground, and stopping just short of you before exhaling a huge whoosh of air. To make this bluff even more effective, the bears would rush through bushes; moving through leaves and branches made more nosie and made them appear larger. In his understated way he said this was disconcerting for the first few times, but he's never actually been attacked.

Above, Black bears can often be seen prowling along salmon streams in Alaska in search of prey
Right, The Vince Shute Sanctuary in Minnesota is home to a community of black bears that remarkably have learnt to trust and tolerate humans

Above, Tree-borne fruit is an important part of the black bear's diet, particularly in summer. The bears use their prehensile tongues and lips to delicately pluck the berries from the branches, without eating any leaves

I hoped I wouldn't be disconcerted as we headed into the forest, taking care not to go too far from the meadow, so the bears didn't forget that away from the sanctuary people can be lethal.

We could hear it before we saw it. In this peaceful forest the noise of splintering wood was tremendous. Pushing our way through dense hazel brush, we came to Norma Jean the bear. She looked up and I thought she may run at me, but she was reassured by the sound of Klarie's voice.

She continued her less-than-delicate dissection of a rotting log, searching the fragments of wood with her curved claws and finger-like toes. Even though they're classified as carnivores, most bears with one exception, eat very little meat. The title is a legacy from the ancestral hunters that gave rise to them. Their weaponry, sharp claws and canine teeth, combined with their great strength, still gives them the option to kill other mammals, but they do that only rarely and even then it's usually only when there is an easy opportunity, in the case of the black bear when they stumble across a new-born deer or moose. The bulk of their diet is vegetables, grasses and herbaceous plants in spring, shrub and tree-borne fruit in summer, and fruit and nuts in autumn. They'll also take insects, as Norma Jean proved from only 2 m (7 ft) away, lassooing succulent white beetle grubs with her remarkably long prehensile tongue and lips. Earlier that week, Bill had

seen Norma Jean dig up a wasp's nest, eating grubs and adults indiscriminately. There is one report of a bear with 0.25 l (half a pint) of wasps in its stomach; it had eaten them whole, stings and all. For me, tent caterpillars seem just as unappetising. They may not sting but they are covered with irritating protective hairs. In other parts of their range, black bears eat these pests in their thousands! Black bears love honey, tearing bees' nests apart, their hides and pelts protecting them from the attacking bees. Although every now and then they shake the enraged insects away as if they're merely droplets of water. They've even been known to climb up telegraph poles to tear the wires down, mistaking their hum for the droning of bees.

Norma Jean finished scrutinizing the remains of the log and ploughed through dense vegetation heading to the meadow. It was hard going keeping up with her. She soon stopped in a clearing and flipped over a huge rock – a reminder of her great power. There was an ant's nest and I was reminded of Baloo the bear's song in Disney's *The Jungle Book*, 'The Bear Necessities'. She thrust a paw into the colony and then proceeded to lick off the ants that crawled onto it!

For the first time since we'd been with her, she was in the sun, and I could see the glossiness of her black pelt. Bill told me that black bears do not have to be jet-black. Although nearly all the Vince Shute bears are black, 12 per cent are cinnamon. In other populations there is more variation and they can be light brown or the colour of cream. There's even a population in a portion of coastal Alaska and British Columbia that has a blue rinse. Black varieties are much more prevalent in moist, forested areas, like the area we were in. It is thought that melanin, the pigment that makes the pelage black, may strengthen the coat, saving it from being worn away as the bear constantly pushes through and past leaves and branches. Also, these forest bears are never too far from deep shade, so keeping cool isn't a problem for them. In more open, arid areas a brown pelage is more prevalent because with less abrasive vegetation, there is no need for such a durable coat, and also the bears are out in the sun more – brown fur absorbs less heat.

Bill beckoned me closer. Norma Jean's shoulder was about 1 m (3 ft) above the ground, the height of my waist. If she stood on her hind legs, she'd be about as tall as I am, 1.9 m (6 ft) tall. Female black bears weigh between 40 and 136 kg (90–300 lb), and she probably weighed about 90 kg (200 lb). The larger males are between 68 and 227 kg (150–500 lb). In 1987 one record breaker was caught, weighed and released at a rubbish tip – he tipped the scales at 364 kg (803 lb).

The supply of ants and their larvae was soon exhausted and we all moved off. I was close; it was as if Norma Jean had invited me into her world, and I tried to imagine being a bear. Their main window on the world is their nose. As we walked, Norma Jean sniffed constantly. For processing scents she has an area of olfactory membrane 100 times greater than mine. Although this is her main sense, she can hear just about as well as I can. She probably can't see quite as well over longer distances, but close up she can see accurately and in colour. A bush of crimson hawthorn berries attracted her now and she used the same paw that I'd seen tear apart solid wood and the same prehensile lips and tongue to delicately pluck off the berries without eating a single leaf.

Black bears must take feeding very seriously, particularly in the northern part of their range. They only have half of the year to put on enough fat to survive the freezing conditions the other half will bring.

In a month or so, Norma Jean would be searching out the concentrated energy of acorns, beech, hickory and hazel nuts. It's extraordinary that the life of such giants is ruled by the distribution and abundance of tiny fruits and nuts. Without them, they won't even breed. Autumn is the critical feeding period. Bears may gain 1.5 kg (3.3 lb) per day, increasing their weight by 30–40 per cent in two months. Their feeding at this time of year is often called the 'fall shuffle' because when foraging for high energy foods, bears may travel great distances. Because of the supplementary diet of corn and dry dog food, fruits, nuts and berries offered at the sanctuary, these bears rarely do.

I could see that Norma Jean was already barrelling out and this year in particular, it was crucial for her to put on weight. If she did, in early winter, cubs would begin to grow inside her. Earlier in the summer, Norma Jean was receptive and she'd mated. Females only mate every other year, because their cubs are dependent on them for 18 months or so.

Although Norma Jean had fertilised embryos, they hadn't developed further than being a ball of cells. Bears delay the development of their embryos for up to five months – a process known as delayed implantation. In November the ball of cells should be

implanted into the wall of the uterus and gestation proper will begin. That's unless there's a scarcity of food – a failure of nut crop, for example – in which case the embryo doesn't implant at all and the female skips breeding that year.

Norma Jean certainly looked corpulent enough for her pregnancy to go ahead. In early October she'd find

Above, A North American black bear can stand 1.9 m (6 ft) tall. Their weight ranges from 40–136 kg (90–300 lb) for females, to 68–227 kg (150–500 lb) for the larger males

Above, In parts of the black bear's range the climate can be extremely hot and humid in summer, and a swim in the water is one way the bear can cool itself down

a den in a rock, cave, crevice or hollow tree. She may even hollow out her own in a brush pile or amongst fallen trees. She would need some insulation from the cold ground during the depths of winter, and to this end, she would scoop up leaves and grass with her front feet, dragging them backwards to the den.

By the end of the month, her winter sleep would begin. She'd curl up into a ball, conserving heat by giving herself as small a surface area as possible, and snuggling her head into the thicker hair of her belly. Scientists describe bears in winter as 'metabolic marvels'. Most hibernators – hedgehogs, dormice, bats and woodchucks – drop their temperature until it is just above freezing and lower their heartbeat and breathing rate, spending periods of time in a sort of 'suspended animation'. Then, every few days, they must wake up to stretch their limbs, perhaps eat or drink and urinate and defecate. This waking-up process is fuelled by special deposits of brown fat. If this process didn't happen, by spring their bodies

would be damaged by the build up of waste products.

Bears have a different strategy. Hibernating males and females without cubs maintain a body temperature of 30°C (88°F), only 7°C (12°F) below the norm in summer. This means they can wake up quickly if disturbed, but if not, they can sleep the whole winter through without drinking, eating or defecating. They survive on their fat reserves and lose a quarter of their weight by spring, but the loss is entirely fat; they do not use up any of their lean body mass the way a starving human would. Bears are the only animals in the world that give birth in the dead of winter when they're starving in this way. After only a two-month gestation, 2–3 cubs would be born. The blind young have such fine hair they appear naked. Snow banked up outside the den makes their nursery seem frigid, but it helps keep it warm. In winter temperatures can drop to minus 30°C (minus 22°F).

Norma Jean's heart rate would drop from around 60 beats per minute to 30 beats, but her body temperature would hover around 38°C (100°F), just a few degrees below what it was currently in summer. Weighing just over 0.45 kg (1 lb), her cubs will need to be kept warm. Nourished by their mother's milk, and warmed in the crevices of her slumbering body, they will be able to stand when they are about four weeks old, at which time they will also open their baby blue eyes.

This extraordinary breeding strategy has been brought about by the young needing a complete spring and summer to fatten up and prepare for the rigours of the winter. They need to be born early in the year when their mothers are hibernating; no other animal does this. The females could not cope with this if they had to give birth to well-developed babies which needed to be kept inside their womb for a longer period – it is not efficient for a hibernating bear to nourish its babies through a placenta. Instead they are born under-developed, and by suckling milk they develop outside the body in a sort of external pregnancy.

In spring, Norma Jean would have lost 40 per cent of her body weight, but her cubs would be about the size of racoons, well co-ordinated and ready to learn from their mother about life in the woods. They'd stay with her for one more winter, gaining their independence in about June at 18 months old. Norma Jean led us back towards the meadow. Following her, I was intrigued by a tassle of fur hanging down between her black legs. Bill explained that this was the best way to identify a female black bear. When she urinated this tassle would soak up the liquid and improve the efficacy of marking her territory when she rubbed her behind over scent posts.

As we came out of the forest other bears I hadn't noticed before had converged upon us. They move so silently through the woods. The excitement of this place made me catch my breath; these were totally wild bears, not hand-reared or injured ones being rehabilitated. I'd spent the day with black bears and I felt I knew them just a little. They have the biggest brain compared to body length of any land animal and from what I'd seen they behave as though they have. Observing their behaviour in the sanctuary, they seemed to show so much trust. This was surely the natural state of affairs before we began to shoot and trap them. I just hoped none of the bears here would fall to a hunter's bullet. Between 4,000 and 6,000 bears become trophies in Minnesota every year.

Black bears rarely use their great strength to attack people. Only 20 people have been killed in the last 100 years. Predation was the motive for most of the deaths and luckily it's a rare black bear indeed that considers a human to be prey. To put this in perspective, for each death from a black bear there are over 90,000 murders.

In recent times, more and more of us are encroaching on their territory, and there have been hundreds of accounts of attacks resulting in minor cuts and bruises. Most black bear-inflicted injuries occur around camp grounds in national parks. Bears get so used to seeking out garbage or being fed that they get irritable and lash out if they're denied. Today, there are strict regulations so the number of incidents should decrease. In Yosemite National Park, black bears turn their great strength to car crime too. Over a three-year period in the 1970s, 1,493 vehicles were damaged by bears seeking food. Visitors could return to find a mangled wreck with smashed windows, and window and door frames pulled out and thrown to the ground. Unfortunately once bears have learnt how to raid cars it is hard to make them stop, so they usually have to be destroyed. The only way to prevent these smash and grab raids is to not leave food in cars at all. These statistics belie the fact that black bears are usually tolerant of people. The population of 4,100 in New York State illustrates this well. Between 1960 and 1980 it is estimated that people spent 77 million recreation days in 'black bear country'. During this whole period there were just three bear-related injuries.

Below, A hungry black bear scavenging from a rubbish bin. Most black bear-inflicted injuries occur around camp grounds in national parks. Bears get so used to seeking out garbage or being fed that they get irritable and lash out if they're denied

Brown Bear

The brown bear has a more dangerous reputation. It is an animal that, in North America at least, is more often found in open habitats where it has only one option for defence, direct aggression. Black bears don't usually have to rely on ferocity – they scramble up trees at the first hint of danger – whereas brown bears can't climb at all. Tree climbing is one of the first skills black bear cubs learn after they've left the den. As they can escape to the forest's upper story for safety, their mother does not need to stand her ground and defend them aggressively – given the chance she'll just follow them up the tree. People injured by black bears usually only have minor cuts. Half of those mauled by brown bears, there have been a couple of hundred cases since the turn of the century, are injured very seriously. Brown bears are so strong they can crush the skull of a bull with a single blow or flip over boulders weighing several hundred pounds. That's why Troy Hurtubise's bear-proof suit will need to be durable.

Even so, most brown bears will flee if they have the opportunity. My 'first' three brown bears in Kumchatka in the far east of Russia, ran as fast as they could when I approached. It was frustrating as I wanted a good view but all I saw was three big, wobbly bottoms with ludicrously small tails disappearing into the distance.

Brown bears are one of the must vulnerable species on earth. As well as the Americas, they were formerly found across a huge swathe of the planet, but now they are irregularly distributed across this range, because of habitat loss and other conflicts with people. Fewer than 150,000 brown bears remain; most of those are in Russia and North America. They can still be found in central and western Europe, although fewer than 500 bears still roam Spain's Cantabrian Mountains, the Pyrenees, the Alps and Italy's Abruzzo Mountains. They are faring better in Scandinavia and eastern Europe, but as you continue eastwards, most of the southern populations are declining. I have looked for them in the Elburz mountains, just three hours' drive from Iran's capital, Tehran. I didn't see them, but a cameraman who had been to the same locality three weeks earlier, had filmed a mother and cubs and the odd single bear every day for a week or so. There is still room for bears in overcrowded Japan – the northern island of Hokkaido has many bears – although they are now at risk from hunting.

Just as black bears aren't necessarily black, brown bears aren't always brown. Even more confusingly, different forms of brown bear can have different common names even though they all belong to the same species.

This is because there is great variation between and within populations, particularly in size and colour. Some bears are blond, more usually they're any shade of brown, but can even be black. Individuals can vary with the season. Bleached by the sun, their coats become lighter, but when they moult in summer, with a new coat, the bear is at its darkest. When the first

Above, On Kodiak Island brown bears are hunted and so are hard to get close to. This is Koda a 7-year old male born in captivity near Vancouver, Canada. He has starred in five feature films and several commercials

settlers reached the western edge of the Rockies, they came across a particularly dark form of brown bear, with white tips to its fur, the original grizzly. Nowadays that name is sometimes given to all American brown bears, and sometimes only to those of the interior, which are often frosted with white or silver giving this grizzled appearance. In Alaska brown bear populations within 120 km (75 miles) of tide water can be called coastal browns. This confusion doesn't arise with European or Asian populations; they are just called brown.

Grizzly is one animal name that makes most people's blood run cold. You would imagine from the fear and awe grizzlies command, that they would also be the largest form of brown bear, but surprisingly the bears on the coast are three times as heavy. To see why these bears are so large, I travelled with a film crew to the coast of Alaska's Katmai National Park. This was real wilderness, so remote the only way in is by boat or a float plane. Our orange De Havilland Beaver flew from Kodiak Island, Alaska, on 18 August. The flight was breathtaking. The coast we skimmed over is often obscured by rain and fog, but the sun shone on this day and beside us, stretching 1,220 m (4,000 ft) into the vault of a flawless blue sky, and seemingly close enough to touch, were the mountains of the Aleutian range. The high valleys were filled with the icy tongues of glaciers, the lower ones blanketed with short tundra vegetation. The shoreline was like the edge of a giant jigsaw piece indented with dramatic fjord-like inlets. As the tide was low a thick brown margin of mud flats delineated the coast proper from the sea. The first clue as to why the bears here are so big came from the birds that we flew over. Even though we were 30 m (100 ft) or so above them, I could see the broad, flat wings, snow-white head and tail, and even the hooked yellow bill. The birds were bald eagles. There are 300 pairs in the Katmai National Park, and they flourish here for the same reason the bears do – salmon.

The float plane dropped us off at our boat *The Waters*, this would be our base for the next six days. Exploration using a boat as a base is the best way to keep this wilderness pristine. Our guide on the appropriate way to behave around wild bears was Buck

Above, The coastal browns are the giants among the species – they benefit from an abundance of protein-packed salmon, whereas brown bears found in the interior of the continent never encounter salmon, and a greater percentage of their diet is salads, fruits and nuts

Wilde, a nature photographer who had been here for the last three summers. We were in a place with the densest population of brown bears anywhere in the world: about 1.6 per sq. km (1 per sq. mile). The park area was 15,540 km (6,000 sq. miles) so there are a good few bears. These coastal browns certainly live up to their name. Their life is governed by the tides, almost as much as the lives of limpets or starfish are. Coming ashore at our first destination, Kukak Bay, we saw the first evidence of bears – holes in the mud. These were definitely excavations as there were spoil piles next to the pits and the surrounding mud was striated by claws. Black bears rarely dig for food. They have short curved claws, whereas the larger species has straighter ones up to 15 cm (6 in) long to help them dig – in this case razor clams were being sought, but brown bears also dig up succulent roots, tubers, corms, bulbs and even ground squirrels. I put my hand in a footprint. It was short and broad – one-and-a-half times the

length of my hand but two-and-a-half times the width. All bears have five toes except the giant panda which has six. Puncture marks made in the mud by the long claws were also obvious. Bears can't retract their claws like cats so these marks are often part of the track. The print made by the hind paw was larger and slimmer, reminding me of my own foot except the 'big toe' was located on the outside of the paw.

For the next few days we filmed young bears running at salmon in the shallow streams and mothers and cubs. We still needed to meet mature male bears and Buck thought he knew where we could do that. The next day we headed for a narrow stream connecting two lakes. Sockeye, the only salmon species to spawn in still water at the edge of lakes, were running the stream now and there weren't too many places to hide from bears. The countryside was ruggedly beautiful, the sun shone, but foreboding grey clouds glowered above the mountain peaks.

It wasn't long before we came upon the bear, a young male perhaps three years old. The tide was coming in but his digging was desultory. When in season salmon are the preferred food. When they are not running this bear could dig 100 holes for shellfish during one low tide and rarely miss.

The incoming tide pushed us and the bear beyond the beach. There we came across a female bear and her cub grazing in the coastal meadows – I was reminded more of cows than meat-eaters. We sat quietly on a log and the pair came towards us. Jeff Goodman filmed over my shoulder as the bears approached. Buck talked to them constantly so our presence wouldn't surprise them. They came so close soundman Mark Roberts was able to record the sound of them pulling up sedge grass and the cub's soft cries. He was asking to be fed and the mother lay on her back like a great furry table and he crawled on her chest to feed, suckling from each of her six teats in turn. What an honour for us this was. I felt we'd been invited into the bear's world.

Meanwhile the other bear we were following looked at us nonchalantly and carried on scrutinizing the stream. He was different to a black bear. His coat was much shaggier, his ears much smaller and he didn't have the straight 'roman nose'. His profile was much more dish-shaped. The biggest difference was the prominent hump on his shoulders. Packed with muscles this is the power house for all that digging brown bears do. His scent was carried to me on the wind. I'll never forget that musky, musty smell.

Right, Female brown bears give birth to and nurse cubs during the winter. The cubs remain with their mother for the first year, learning how to find food

About 30 m (98 ft) away from the bear, there was a commotion in the shallows. Rapids grumbled further upstream and it seemed that before negotiating the faster flowing water, the salmon backed up here. Suddenly the bear moved its great bulk with alacrity. I knew they could run at 56 kph (35 mph) but when there's one coming straight for you, it seems much quicker. The water boiled with salmon as he flew into the shoal. Archimedes wouldn't have needed that bath if he'd seen this! Two walls of water exploded from either side of the bear. I thought the salmon were going to be left high and dry. It all happened so fast I couldn't work out whether he'd grabbed a fish with his long claws before transferring it to his mouth or whether he'd bitten into it straight away. Next to me the cameraman had a more magnificent view. Looking through the camera and down the lens, his whole field of view was filled with galloping, pouncing bear. Even when we reviewed the processed film back in Bristol, we still couldn't see exactly how the fish was caught. That afternoon the action was obscured by an explosion of water. We saw the bear gorge on a dozen more salmon before the storm broke and we had to retreat to the boat.

I knew this bear we'd been filming was a male by his tremendous bulk. Even though they're only 10–15 per cent longer than females, males weigh 1.5–2 times as much. Size varies between populations of brown bears. These coastal ones are the giants of the species. The world record animals are found on Kodiak Island, less than 64 km (40 miles) away. Katmai bears can be 2.7 m (9 ft) from nose to tail, weighing more than 771 kg (1,700 lb).

The largest bears are found in Alaska because of equable weather and a huge reserve of food. There are thousands of fruiting plants such as salmonberries, blueberries and elderberries, all nourished by the mild moist climate. Kodiak is known as Alaska's 'emerald isle' and is as green as anywhere on Earth; temperatures are usually around 21°C (70°F) in summer and seldom fall to 0°C (32°F) in winter. Of course, there are berries in the interior of the continent as well, but bears found in the interior never encounter salmon, their diet is mainly salads, fruits and nuts. It is these protein- and fat-rich fish that make the difference between a big brown bear and a giant.

Above, Despite the fear they instill, brown bears are one of the most vulnerable species on earth. Formerly found across a huge swathe of the planet, they are now irregularly distributed and their numbers have declined to less than 150,000

Polar Bear

One species of bear, the biggest land carnivore on the planet feeds almost exclusively on marine mammals, the only bear that eats mainly meat. It usually catches its seals alive.

It is probable that sometime in the last 250,000–100,000 years some brown bears travelled north along the Arctic coast. Many of them perished but some survived on scavenged seal carcasses. Eventually some of them learnt to stalk and kill seals and over the millennia they slowly transformed into a new kind of bear: the polar bear. In evolutionary terms this happened rapidly and the largest bear of all is fairly young as species go. In fact, the genetic distance between polar bears and their brown bear ancestors, is still so close that in captivity they will interbreed and produce fertile hybrids.

The polar bear was and still is the first marine bear; it depends on the ocean for its existence. Once those first bears had ventured out into the sea, the changes they underwent enhanced their survival there. From then on, the backdrop of snow and ice was the one they were most often seen against, and to blend in with their surroundings they became white. They also became relentless killers – to survive at all they needed to eat flesh. Their snouts and neck became longer and there were changes inside their mouths too. Instead of short canine teeth they developed long sharp ones; the other teeth became narrow, ragged and sharp. These modifications led to a better design for tearing seals apart.

I'd seen the imprint made by long curved claws on the beach at Katmai. This trademark of a brown bear footprint is lacking in polar bears who have short stocky claws which are probably less likely to break through unforgiving ice. Polar bears also became giants in bear terms. Black bears are a third of their size; most populations of brown bears are also much smaller, although those from the Alaskan island of Kooknak can grow nearly as huge. This is because energy conservation is more efficient in a larger body than a smaller one – an important factor for polar bears which spend most of their lives exposed to the bitter cold of

the Arctic. Today there are between 25,000 and 40,000 polar bears in the frozen north. They usually inhabit the ice-covered waters of half a dozen countries: Canada, Denmark, Norway, Russia, Iceland and the United States. Given a choice, they would stay on the sea all year round but like sea birds, females usually have to come ashore to breed. There's also one unique group of bears that is trapped on the land between July and November every year. They are the most southerly polar bears in the world (except those in captivity), reaching the latitude of the Midlands in Britain, and form the world's densest population – about 1,200 of them gather in a narrow strip along the western shore of Hudson Bay in Manitoba, Canada. Slap-bang in the middle of this polar bear colony is the port of Churchill, a town surrounded by miles of tundra. The port was established to transport prairie grain by boat and train to other areas, but it is the bears that have made it famous. Churchill looks just as a wilderness settlement should. It boasts the second largest stone fort in North America, and flat-roofed prefabricated buildings line the streets, most with a snowmobile parked outside. An airfield and train station make the polar bears of Churchill the most accessible in the world. Journeys from Winnipeg take four hours by plane, or a night, a day and another night by train. There are also two or three motels in Churchill, so that when your encounters are over you can spend the night in comfort. All the motels are as warm as toast, an important consideration in late autumn when you become chilled to the bone in minutes as soon as you venture out into the street. That is not quite all you

Right, the imposing bulk of an adult polar bear can only really be appreciated when up close. Their huge powerful paws are used for dragging seals out of the water. They also distribute the bear's weight so that it can walk on surprisingly thin ice and are used as highly efficient paddles when swimming

Above, Only 30 m (98 ft) away two huge males reared up to spar. For a second there was a face-off. They stood 2 m (6 ft) apart on their hind legs with their forelegs hanging limply. I was watching a ritualised play fight

need, as the film crew and I found out when we met up with our guide Denis. He was perched high above the ground at the wheel of one of the strangest vehicles I'd ever seen. We clambered aboard the tundra buggy, from the outside it looked like a creation from the *Mad Max* movies; inside it was comfortable and mercifully heated and it even had a toilet. Len Smith, a Churchill resident, developed these machines which are made from the scavenged body parts of old farm machinery. Their most important components are their agricultural tyres, 91 cm (3 ft) across and 1.83 m (6 ft) tall. We soon found out why tundra buggies have to be both tough and high.

We headed straight across the tundra, lumbering over hillocks and gravel banks, and plunging through fractured ice up to our axles in the mud of shallow lakes. Gordon Point was our destination, a peninsula of land jutting into Hudson Bay. Even though the wind whipped over the water, the waves were not moving as quickly as we might have thought; congealing ice slowed them down, it wouldn't be long before the sea froze over.

Gordon Point was bleak. The wind had swept most of the snow away and our wheels crunched over sand and gravel. We passed trees of a sort, dwarf willows 1.21 m (4 ft) high or less. We hadn't come for the scenery,

Below centre, The bears' long, snake-like necks weaved about as each looked for an opening to gain an advantage over the other. The fighting males also used their mouths but there was little power in their bites and no blood was drawn **Bottom**, The bout lasted for about three minutes until both bears slid to the ground. There they continued wrestling and I was reminded of two great puppy dogs at play. One of the bears was pinned on its back, and while the other gently gnawed at its neck, it ineffectually pedalled its back legs in the air as if it was being tickled

however, we'd come for polar bears and here we found a dozen or more. This was the first time I'd seen one of the most charismatic animals on the planet and I was not disappointed.

Only 30 m (98 ft) away two huge males reared up to spar. For a second there was a face-off. They stood 2 m (6 ft) apart on their hind legs with their forelegs hanging limply. Then, almost in slow motion, one of them fell forwards, concentrating his power in a single thump that sent ice particles from his adversary's coat exploding into the frigid air. Their long, snake-like necks weaved about as each looked for an opening, then they locked in an embrace which must have given us the expression 'bear hug'. I was watching a ritualised play fight,. This could be designed to get the muscles toned up after the forced inactivity of the summer months, or it could be a way that males assess the strengths and weaknesses of opponents before the serious fights over females begin. Mating happens out on the sea ice in late winter or spring. Because cubs remain with their mothers for two and a half years, females only breed every three years. This means that in the breeding season only one third of the females will be receptive. There is intense competition for them, with the biggest, heaviest males having most chance of success, which is why they grow to such an impressive size. The fighting males also used their mouths but there was little power in their bites and no blood was drawn. The bout lasted for about three minutes until both bears slid to the ground. There they continued wrestling and I was reminded of two great puppy dogs at play. One of the bears was pinned on its back, and while the other gently gnawed at its neck, it ineffectually pedalled its back legs in the air as if it was being tickled. The temperature was about 0°C (32°F), a warm day for polar bears, and the exertion had obviously taken it out of them and they turned over and fell asleep.

We didn't have to wait long for more action. A mother with two yearling cubs walked towards us over a frozen pond. We thought they may investigate the buggy but she veered away towards the shore line. Even so, we achieved a good film sequence of the family which gave us a chance to show that polar bears aren't really that white. In full sunlight the mother was the yellow of the curds of whey that are found in clotted cream. The cubs were shaded in ivory and pearl. Polar bears actually have translucent fur which takes on different colours by the refraction of sunlight (the

same phenomenon that makes clouds appear white). The fur can get stained in older animals which is why they appear yellow. They seem at their whitest just after a moult.

I really saw how extraordinary their coats are when we filmed an anaesthetised bear. Churchill has a friendly war with bears which have taken to entering the town limits. Given a chance they would brazenly forage in bins right in the centre. They must be dissuaded, because if you walk down the street and surprise one, both you and the bear will get a nasty fright. Close encounters between people and frightened bears are extremely dangerous, one or the other can be killed. In these situations local armed police usually ensure that the bear comes off worse. To avoid this happening a bear patrol traps and darts offending bears. They are then taken to the polar bear jail – an old aeroplane hanger just out of town. The captives are kept inside small cages and given nothing but water. This sounds cruel, but apart from the odd berry or scrap of seaweed, there is no natural food in the surrounding area until the bears can get back out on the sea ice. Hopefully the fright of being incarcerated is a potent enough lesson, so when they're taken in a net slung under a helicopter to a remote part of the bay, they won't come back to town again.

Lying next to a sleeping bear just before release, I could run my hands through its fur. The long translucent guard hairs were so hard and shiny they appeared synthetic. They are hollow and act as light pipes, funnelling solar radiation to the black skin to be absorbed as heat (yes, a shaved polar bear is black). By parting the guard hairs I could feel the under layer of dense fur just like the wool of a sheep.

Stroking a bear also made me realise how small I was by comparison. Stretched out this female bear was 2 m (6.5 ft) long, 10 cm longer that I am tall, and she was much more solidly built, weighing 260 kg (573 lb), three times my weight. The discrepancy between me and the male bear would be even greater. In 1960, a male was shot on Kotzebue Sound, Alaska that weighed 1,002 kg (2,210 1b) and stood 3.4 m (11 ft 2 in) tall, but this was exceptional. Adult males weigh on average 400–600 kg (880–1,323 lb), and measure about 2.4 m (7 ft 10 in) from nose to tail, but as I found out, their ability to stand upright means that to be safe, the windows of a tundra buggy have to be very high indeed.

After the mother and her cubs had disappeared along the beach we moved further up Gordon Point.

Left, a tranquilised bear is taken in a net slung under a helicopter to a remote part of the bay. Hungry bears have to be removed from towns in this way to prevent potentially dangerous encounters with humans

Below, before it was transported away from Churchill I was able to get really close to this tranquilised polar bear. Underneath the hard, shiny guard hairs there is a thick layer of dense fur. Beneath that the polar bear's skin is black

Before long, a single bear ran straight toward us, Denis was pretty sure it was a sub-adult male. Our first impression was one of awkwardness. Rising higher than his shoulders, his rump swayed from side to side and he had a lolloping gait. His back feet looked as if they were going to run into his front ones, but all these components somehow worked efficiently together and he moved fast, flowing over the ice with supple agility. I turned to talk to the cameraman, and the next thing I knew there was a grunt and a thump, and a black nose appeared in the window. I looked into the bear's slightly bloodshot brown eyes from less than 30 cm (12 in) away. He was on us, and standing 3 m (10ft) above the ground in a flash; how could I have thought he was clumsy? Bears should never be underestimated. The window was open so we didn't have to film through the glass with the problems of condensation, scratches and smears. The inquisitive bear put its great paw through the gap. Only tiny areas of the pads of the feet were visible. They were covered by fur for insulation and to help grip on to the ice. Without a microscopic examination I couldn't see the extraordinary structure of the pads themselves. Scientists have found that soft papillae protrude from the surface, their function

being to increase the friction between the foot and the ice. There are also small depressions, which may act like suction cups, enhancing the efficacy of polar bears' non-slip soles even more.

This unique design could help prevent industrial accidents; every year more than a million injuries are caused by people slipping over. Designers have looked at polar bear paw pads to see if any of their features could be adopted for shoes to make them safer.

The bear scraped his foot along the window frame, the pads were carried underneath a paw that was nearly 25 cm (10 in) across. Its great feet help the bear in a number of ways. First, they are used as paddles for swimming. Secondly, they work as snow and ice shoes, spreading the weight of the animal so that it doesn't sink down into the snow or break through the ice. Thirdly, a bear can use its paw as a club for battering prey. As our bear strained to get its leg further into the buggy, that last purpose was uppermost in my mind; if a bear can drag a seal through its breathing hole breaking every bone in its body in the process, pulling me through a window shouldn't be that difficult. I was glad tundra buggies had been designed with hungry bears in mind.

At this time of the year, in November, all of the bears around Churchill are hungry as they've eaten virtually nothing since July. They are waiting for Hudson Bay to freeze over so they have a platform to hunt from once more. That is why bears congregate around Churchill; because of fresh water flowing into the sea, coastal ice forms earliest here. They're ill at ease on the land and it seemed to me that all the milling about, jousting, thrilling tourists and film crews were ways of marking time until they could quit the coast. In the summer they'd have been very uncomfortable. Overheating is a problem for them, and to avoid it they have dug sleeping pits, sometimes right down to the permafrost to get out of direct sunlight. Ironically, the hungrier they get, the less overheating is a problem, as the blubber they stored over the hunting season gets eaten away for nourishment. Now their impatience to leave was almost tangible, but they wouldn't have to wait long. When we flew out from Churchill four days later on 20 November, there was no sea to be seen – Hudson Bay had frozen over completely. From the aeroplane we could even see some creamy flecks on the blue grey ice, many of the bears had already left the land.

Only polar bears that are pregnant den up for the winter, the rest spend their time out on the sea ice. The pregnant females have a tremendous ordeal ahead of them. They make their way to a denning area between the Nelson and Churchill areas. Here, like all expectant polar bears, they will excavate an upwardly-sloping den, 61 cm (24 in) wide and 1.5–3 m (5–10 ft) long, which widens out into a chamber just big enough for a bear to turn around. The cavern also has a hole to the surface for ventilation. These dens are not just simple burrows; bears must take care in choosing the right site and they perfect and modify the design even during the winter. The thickness of the snow walls and the air flow are all important. The temperature inside hovers at around 32°C (90°F), whatever the temperature outside, and the bear herself generates about as much heat as a 200-watt light bulb. Her heartbeat drops from 60 beats a minute to 30, but she'll wake up if it gets too warm. If that happens, the walls melt and then refreeze. This layer of ice stops the exchange of oxygen and carbon dioxide, so the female scrapes the ice away or may even have to build a new den.

The dens soon become nurseries. In January all over the Arctic polar bear mothers give birth. The commonest litter size is two; a single cub is rare and triplets rarer still. This is a difficult time for all polar

bear mothers. The summer months are lean times but most populations can usually find some ice and associated food. Remarkably, when Churchill females give birth, they haven't eaten a substantial meal for six months and they must survive on stored fat for another two to three months while they nurse their cubs.

Polar bear cubs must grow faster than other bear babies because of the extreme cold when they leave the den and, unlike brown and black bears, they will not spend the following winter in a den. Instead they must be strong enough to follow their mother as she hunts out on the sea ice. To this end polar bear milk is incredibly rich; 33 per cent fat it has the consistency of cream. The fat content of brown and black bears milk is only 22 per cent. The cubs weigh less than 1 kg (2 lb 8 oz) at birth, and by the time they enter the Arctic world outside the den in March or April, they weigh 10 times as much.

It was mid-April when I had my first experience of the world polar bear cubs totter into. I hoped my hi-tech winter gear would protect me in the way that hundreds and thousands of years of evolution had prepared the polar bears. The temperature was minus 20°C (minus 4°F). Only my eyes were exposed but they

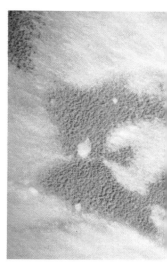

Top and centre, Vehicles such as the Tundra Buggy are one of the few ways you can safely see polar bears up close. Footprints on fresh snow are often one of the first indications that polar bears are in the area

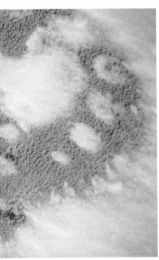

stung from the cold and the ice particles hurled into them by the wind. Except for their nose and eyes, fur covers every part of a polar bear. Unlike them, I had to keep my nose covered too due to it being fleshier than a bear's and completely unsuited to seriously freezing conditions. Until now I hadn't really understood what wind-chill really meant. It is the cooling effect of wind on bare skin exposed to different cold temperatures. The greater the wind, the greater the cooling effect and the colder it feels. The wind was gusting at 48 kph (30 mph) – under these conditions the wind-chill is minus 48°C (minus 52°F) and if my nose was exposed the flesh would freeze in less than a minute.

A hat and a wind-proof balaclava protected my head and most importantly my ears. In proportion to their size polar bears have the smallest ears of any bear, another Arctic adaptation; small extremities have less surface area so they lose less heat. I will never forget the bone-numbing cold. Remarkably the cubs and the adults not only cope with the Arctic conditions but even find them comfortable.

Spitzbergen is the biggest island on Norway's Svalbard archipelago. It is 1,000 km (621 miles) from the North Pole and the Arctic Circle begins 2,000 km (1,243 miles) to the south. Churchill may be the best place in the world for sheer number of polar bears, but comparatively they are slimline giants – most have lost at least a third of their body weight from fasting. To see really big bears you need to find them on their feeding

Right, standing on its hind legs the bear was able to peer through the window. I looked into the bear's slightly bloodshot brown eyes from less than 30 cm (12 in) away. He was standing 3 m (10ft) above the ground

grounds and Spitzbergen is one of the best places in the world to do that. That is because there are many hunting bears, and the area of ice on and around the island is big, but not vast. The self-contained Churchill bears hunt on Hudson Bay, an area of ice the size of Texas.

Spitzbergen is also excellent for bear watching because the animals are well-studied, you can get transport right to the heart of their territory, and with luck you could be with bears two days after leaving London. Planes land daily in Longyearbyen, the island's main town, if the weather permits. Camerman Martin Saunders, soundman Roger Long and I, lost two days due to the inclement weather which we spent in Tromsø, northern Norway. Our plane had to turn back after a strong wind buffeted us so strongly on our descent that it prevented us from landing. From Tromsø, it should be a one or two day trip by snowmobile right into the heart of bear country. The feeding grounds vary from year to year depending upon the distribution of ice. In most years bears have frequented Kvalvåjen (Whale Bay) on the east coast and that is where naturalist and Arctic specialist Matts Forsberg aimed to take us.

I had never been on a snowmobile before, a machine similar to an overweight motorcycle on a pair of skis. It was moments like these when I realised that on this expedition I was constantly being thrown in at the deep end. Now, I was going to have to spend many hours astride a snowmobile. They're great fun once you master how to balance them, but our journey took longer than usual, because we were carrying a load that made the vehicles even more unstable. Behind each machine there was a sled with provisions and, crucially, fuel. There are no petrol stations on the ice and planning fuel supplies is one of the most important factors in an Arctic expedition.

I turned my snow scooter over before we had even left Longyearbyen and then again as we travelled along the side of an incline. That was more serious as rather than being crushed by the falling machine, I jumped clear to see my sled and scooter head straight for a ravine. We all watched aghast. They narrowly avoided boulders that would have crumpled them, and eventually stopped just in front of the chasm. After that I soon worked out how to lean my weight into a slope and avoided tipping over again.

Heated handle bars were a comfort, but provided little real warmth as our average speed was 40 kph (25

mph), and we therefore generated our own wind-chill. To protect ourselves we wore many layers of clothing and goggles over our eyes. We made an enforced stop at the mining town of Sveyar because of a blizzard that lasted for two days causing another delay. When the wind and snow abated we crossed a fjord and climbed onto the crumpled ice of a glacier.

I'm glad we made frequent stops to film. Snow scooters don't give you the smoothest of rides and my body ached with the constant strain of holding a position as we bounced over the uneven ice. The ride was physically demanding but never tiring. I was energised by the grandeur of the landscape: there were infinite variations on a stark theme of snow, ice and blue sky. The inexorable pressure of trundling glaciers contrasted with jagged crevasse fields where abstract sculptures of jade-coloured ice marked the tops of voids that could swallow up a line of a hundred snowmobiles – beautiful but potentially dangerous, just like the polar bears we were searching for. It must have been from landscapes like these that the world's advertising agencies found their symbols of freshness and purity. We rode along the base of a blue glacial wall which towered 30 m (90 ft) high and was shot through with streaks of green ice like bars of coloured soap.

Seven days after leaving Britain, and four days later than we anticipated, we reached our destination – a wooden hut nestled at the base of a high rounded hill. It was 10 o'clock at night but we didn't need torches to unload in the gloaming; this far north it would not get fully dark for another four months. From the last week in April the sun never dips below the horizon. The frozen sea of Whale Bay was little more than a stone's throw away and we were only on the edge of the nature reserve.

Polar bears are frequent along this stretch of coast, particularly in the nature reserve but snowmobiles aren't permitted there. You are allowed in if you use your own muscle power, but neither the crew or myself were accomplished cross-country skiers, and even using the hut as a base camp for superfluous film equipment, we still needed to take with us 100 kg (220 lb) of gear for normal day-to-day filming. We also needed to cover a vast amount of ground. A single polar bear may have a home range twice as big as the country of Iceland, and can walk steadily at about 6 kph (4 mph). We could never hope to keep up on our own. That is why we enlisted the strength and stamina of other creatures, animals that aren't excluded from any part of Spitsbergen, and which epitomise the Arctic as much as the great white bear we were seeking. They were huddled in depressions in the snow. Some had ice-matted fur, some were black, some brown, others white. All of the huskies greeted us. Their owners, dog mushers Talia and Bjorn, had left a couple of days before us to dig the snow away from the hut and to repair the damage that had been done by a ransacking bear. The first rule with any of these huts is never to leave any food behind – the temptation for a bear is just too great.

For the next four days, the weather was glorious and we searched for polar bears. Outside the nature reserve we used the snowmobiles, but inside dog sleds were the order of the day. It was a most exhilarating way to travel. The sleds seemed flimsy as basically you just sat on a seat with your legs wrapped in sacking and your behind just off the ground. I felt like a pensioner in a bath chair when the final layer of insulation was wrapped around my legs – the hide of a reindeer. One of the dog mushers stood behind the contraption and when we were ready to go, released a metal anchor that until then held the dogs back by biting into the snow. This was essential as the dogs love to run so much that if they manage to take off without a musher behind them, they'd disappear into the Arctic wastes without a second glance. With a musher to guide them they behaved impeccably, a series of calls and whistles turning them right or left, making them go faster or slowing them down. A team can attain speeds of over 35 kph (22 mph). What a way to travel! We swept past glaciers and mountains even negotiating the bumpy pack ice. The most remarkable thing for a naturalist was the way the dogs could defecate when running at full pelt, without stopping to squat on the ground. It was fascinating as long as a fusillade of the stuff didn't hit you in the face.

I really began to get an impression of the polar bear's world, a world that forms in the days of shortening light, but would disappear in early summer. Already the confection of snow and ice was patchy – huge rocks were revealed on the shore and close up I could see gardens of lichens sealed in by a sheet of ice, as if they were preserved in plastic. The wind had lifted the snow cover from some of the hilltops to reveal grey talus slopes. These would seethe with sea birds later in the year. Early fulmars (the Arctic variety has much greyer plumage than the subspecies around our coasts) made their mournful cries as they flew overhead to prospect nest sites.

Polar bears would make short forays on the land for carrion or the odd sea bird, but mostly they walked on the frozen sea. Looking at the vast blue-white expanse it was hard to believe that this was an ocean. Shards of ice protruded into the sky, there were smooth blocks and jagged shapes, and every so often cones of the stuff formed into the shape of a perfect volcano. These contorted forms were so unlike the smooth curves of waves, wavelets and ripples we observe on the sea, but this landscape was created by the sea, and would soon be sea again.

This spring polar bears weren't forthcoming. We even tried camping out (that night the temperature dropped to minus 30°C (minus 22°F)) to see if the dogs and dog food would engage the curiosity of a passing bear, but this wasn't to be. We found tracks but most of them were old; the freshest went up to the brow of a hill where they disappeared. There was a giant drag mark down the other side. It seemed as if this bear had walked up and rolled down. Adult polar bears are known to be playful, and sliding down snow slopes is one of their favourite games. Bjorn told me that he has seen multiple paw and slide marks where a bear had walked up and tobogganed down over and over again.

In Churchill there were plenty of bears with no scenery to speak of. In Spitzbergen, where at least there were magnificent landscapes, we hadn't seen any polar bears. Our time was running out, but we had heard that a few days before that were bears at Tempelfjorden just two hours from Longyearbyen, but were they still there? We packed up to find out.

The situation looked promising as soon as we entered Tempelfjorden; there were black shapes on the ice – ringed seals. On the coast we'd seen none, but they are the main food of polar bears, so we hoped that where we found the prey we could find the predator. Ringed seals play an important role in making polar bears into giants and we wanted to film them too. Weighing 50–70 kg (110–154 lb), ringed seals are the smallest in the Arctic, roughly half the weight of other northern seals. They are also the most abundant and during April tens of thousands of ringed seal pups are born on the ice. We spotted one with the aid of binoculars, but remarkably, polar bears can smell them from 32 km (20 miles) away. The plan was that I would try to approach it from one side, and the film crew from the other, but our chances of getting close shots were slim; ringed seals are very wary, and disappear at the slightest hint of danger. I started from over 200 m (600 ft) away and wriggled forward on my belly. A slow stalk, just like I was doing, is one of the huge number of hunting strategies employed by polar bears. Semi-crouched they edge patiently forward; an explosive, final charge comes when they are 15–30 m (50–100 ft) away. I only hoped I could get that close, particularly as I wasn't as well camouflaged as a polar bear – in fact my jacket was bright orange.

What I was crawling over was a relatively permanent platform. Ringed seals live on sea ice which is anchored to the coastline, not on offshore pack ice, as other Arctic seals do. Sea ice is a relatively stable environment compared to the floating pack ice which shifts and breaks up, so that when the seal pups are born they run the risk of being dumped into the freezing water as their home drifts away. That's why pack ice seals wean their babies so rapidly; harp seals take just twelve days while hooded seals nurse for only four. These are the seal babies that you can easily walk up to as they lay indolently waiting to be fed by their mothers. They're the species of seal that hunters club to death for their pelts. They're so trusting because out on the pack ice predators are few and far between. Polar bears concentrate on the shore-fast ice where the ringed seals are. That's why ringed seals are so wary. If the female seal had spotted me or a polar bear she'd have grabbed her pup by the scruff of the neck and dragged it into the water for safety. Laboriously, I managed to get within 75 m (246 ft) of the pup. It had taken over an hour and my legs were blocks of ice but it was so exhilarating. Every so often the female seal would pop out of her hole to nurse the pup. When she did I stopped crawling and laid still not moving a muscle. Her body glistened in the watery sun and I could see the black rings on her coat that give these seals their name. The pup was covered in white fur. As they live on such stable ice suckling would go on for 4–6 weeks. The baby was a day or two old with very little blubber but just before weaning it could be 75 per cent fat.

In another hour I was extraordinarily close, just 10 m (33 ft) away, and I watched the adult scraping with its front flippers at the perimeter of its ice hole. In pack ice there is ample open water for seals to come to the surface to breathe, but this isn't the case on permanent ice. The ringed seal is unique in its ability to scratch holes in the ice with its sturdy front claws, sometimes through ice as thick as 2 m (6.5 ft).

As well as the seal accepting my presence this situation was unusual in another respect. Pups are rarely exposed as this one was. Snow builds up over many breathing holes so a pup usually has a snow cave for a nursery. Polar bears can smell these from half a mile away even if they're under 1 m (3 ft) of snow. They use another hunting strategy to catch these hidden pups. Moving carefully a short distance at a time they constantly smell the air while listening for any movement. In this way they pinpoint the exact location of the pup within the snow cave, which can be 3.5 m (11 ft) long and 2.5 m (8 ft) wide. Once directly over their prey they bring all four feet to a point

centred over the pup, crashing through the ceiling of the lair in a single pounce. Most attempts aren't successful. The snow may be too hard-packed or the seals are forewarned and seek refuge in another snow cave or breathing hole. They usually have three or four within 100 m (328 ft) of each other.

Polar bears catch adult seals as well, but again a low percentage of hunts are successful. However, polar bears are persistent. There are so many seals that if they miss one there will soon be another to catch. They stalk and then charge a seal when it hauls itself out of an ice hole, or they wait patiently, ready to strike with a single calculated blow from a 18 kg- (40 lb-) paw when a seal comes up to draw breath. Seals are usually safe in the water, easily outswimming a bear.

If a bear makes a kill and it is already healthy and well fed, it will only eat the blubber, leaving the rest of the carcass for hungrier bears or arctic foxes, which out on the sea ice are entirely dependent upon these leftovers. By gorging in this way, bears can consume as much as 2 kg (4 lb) of fat in a day. It is this remarkable adaptation, the ability to store immense amounts of fat when food is around and then burn it up when there is nothing to eat, that makes polar bears into giants. Polar bears are relentless hunters and great opportunists, and will even catch beluga whales. Although these are small whales, they can still measure 4.6 m (15 ft) long and weigh up to 1.6 tonnes. Sometimes they get iced in and a savsatt or small hole in the ice is the only place they can come up to breathe. Polar bears wait for them, and a large male can stun them with a swipe of its paw, and then use its great strength to haul the body onto the ice.

I hoped that this mother and pup would survive, but judging from the way they'd let me get so close, it was unlikely. We'd achieved a magical sequence of me and the polar bear's main prey but we still hadn't found a bear. That evening we did come across the fresh remains of a seal and for Matts this was proof that bears were still hunting here. The next morning we followed some tracks that seemed new. After a while we lost them, but as we scanned the ice blocks at the base of a blue glacier at the end of the fjord, one of them moved. It was a polar bear fidgeting as it slept. I wanted to shout with joy, but as we'd been through blizzards, camped out in temperatures of minus 30°C (minus 22°F) and travelled a long way for this, I couldn't make a sound in case I frightened the bear. Bjorn, one of the mushers, had experienced many encounters with bears

Below, To reach the heart of bear country in Spitzbergen the only way to travel is by snowmobile. Once we reached the nature reserve however, huskies took over the job of transporting us and our equipment across the snow and ice

that were curious about his huskies, nearly always approaching closely and even playing with dogs released from the harness and allowed to run free. It would be a great bonus if we could film this behaviour and a well fed giant bear, but unfortunately neither of these things came about. In my excitement this bear seemed a monster, even a record-breaker but Matts said it was barely a teenager and not even old enough to sex with any certainty. Females reach maximum size in 5–6 years, males in 8–10 by which time they have much wider heads. Even if this youngster had been feasting on seal pups it wouldn't be any heavier than the big starved males I'd seen in Churchill.

Much to Bjorn's surprise, it also wasn't interested in playing with huskies. It allowed us to approach within 15 m (50 ft) or so, then sniffed the air imperiously, turned around on its ice block, lowered its behind and produced a scat, before ambling off beneath the glacier. I was still elated: how many other people can say they've sat behind a team of huskies with the ultimate Arctic animal just over their shoulder?

Lizards

The top three giants among lizards belong to the monitor family, and all are found in south-east Asia. Probably the most famous and formidable is the Komodo dragon, a species which can attain a length of over 3 m (10 ft) and weigh up to 70 kg (154 lb). A carnivore which can kill and devour an entire buffalo with incredible ease, the Komodo is so gigantic that it is even capable of preying on people if they are small and unable to defend themselves.

Lizards are arguably the showiest of reptiles. Many are brightly coloured, their scales blotched, striped or spangled in greens, yellows, blues, reds or purples. Others are adorned with bizarre accoutrements, such as casques, crests, spines, even gaudy throat pouches that can be flashed like banners. But for most of these designer reptiles, small is beautiful. There are about 3,000 species living today and only about half a dozen exceed the 1.8 m (6 ft) mark in length with probably not more than 100 more exceeding 1 m (3 ft). Many of these larger species attain their length at the expense of bulk and are slimline with long, thin tails; they may even be legless and more closely resemble snakes than lizards.

The climate of Britain isn't conducive for a long list of these sun-loving reptiles and we have only three species, the common and sand lizards and the slow worm. The 15–24 cm (6–10 in) sand lizard is the heaviest, and the 30–50 cm (12–20 in) limbless, snakelike slow worm is the longest. To see what group it belongs to you just need to look closely at its beautiful red eyes and wait for them to be covered by an eyelid – a snake's eyes are lidless which means they cannot blink.

Moving further south into Europe the number and variety of lizards increases and for me this is one of the greatest joys of Mediterranean holidays. From boyhood until the present day, the thrill of seeing a lizard darting after an insect, chasing another lizard, or simply basking in the sun, flattening its body to absorb the maximum amount of heat, never diminishes. Lizard watching is best in the spring when it doesn't get too hot or on summer mornings when the sun isn't too high. Lizards like all reptiles rely on external heat sources to keep their bodies functioning. If the air temperature isn't warm enough, they absorb the sun's heat directly by basking, or indirectly from warm objects such as rocks that are around them. If it gets too hot they must seek shade, and if you watch those walls or ruins for long enough, you can see the lizards move between sun and shadow to keep their body temperature just right. The term 'cold-blooded' is misleading as in tropical climates, or if the sun is

shining in temperate ones, reptiles can have a temperature as high as, or even higher than birds or mammals.

Europe's largest lizards are both found in the extreme south of the region, and my first experience took place in southern Spain when I was 14 years old. The warm air, laden with aromatic oils from rock rose and thyme, crackled with the electronic buzz of cicadas. Suddenly a powerful lizard dislodged some pebbles while scurrying between boulders on a dry stone wall, and the excitement made my senses filter out everything except that rock crevice. I ran towards the space through which the lizard had crept – was it going to lead to an underground burrow? Were the rocks too large to dislodge or, if I did manage to move them, would the whole structure collapse and crush the lizard beneath them? I could just see the lizard's tail so I thought I should be able to catch it if I carefully removed one rock at a time. Beads of sweat formed on my face as I worked and after half an hour of painstaking labour just the two lower rocks remained. I pulled one away, simultaneously thrusting my hand into the gap that I'd made, and found myself clasping the muscular body of the lizard. Its powerful jaws opened with a slight hiss and I quickly shifted my grip to just behind its head so it couldn't turn to bite me.

The creature I pulled out into the light was gorgeous. About 80 cm (32 in) long, and nearly half of that length was tail, the eyed lizard (also known as an ocellated lizard) was painted with the palette of a Picasso painting: a vivid green with a row of large blue splodges, bluer than the sky, along either side of its body. Its mouth open and huge muscles strained inside the pink interior and on the lizard's neck; given the

slightest chance it would bite hard. The teeth are quite small but they would certainly draw blood. This species is powerful enough to feed on small rodents and birds, although it usually crushes insects. It can even crack open armoured snails. I put the wall back together as best I could; the cleft was a temporary shelter for the lizard rather than a permanent residence, so I hadn't endangered its security. After this close encounter I released the lizard back onto the wall.

Europe's other large lizard is a legless kind, reminiscent of a giant slow worm, and it's some 1.2–1.3 m (4 ft) long. Adult sheltopusiks or glass snakes are shiny brown and stiff-bodied, lacking the flexibility of snakes, their lookalikes. I first found these on a family holiday to Yugoslavia but since then I've seen them in many of the warmer parts of Eastern Europe including the Greek island of Corfu. They are carnivores and have much the same diet as eyed lizards, although as they are not as fast, slow-moving snails are a particular favourite with them.

Just as cold temperatures reduce the diversity of lizards found in a particular country, any climates that are less than hot will limit their size, and this is one of the main reasons giant lizards are found in tropical climates. They take a long time to warm up, and body temperature needs to be consistently high for them to stay active, and for them to perform vital bodily functions such as the digestion of food. When I first started travelling as a young boy, I regarded eyed lizards and sheltopusiks as being large, even formidable. European lizards are dwarves in comparison to tropical ones, one of which is so powerful it has the capability of preying on people if they are small and unable to defend themselves.

Perentie Monitor

Nearly all of these giant lizards belong to one family, the monitors. The most likely explanation of how this name came about goes back to a German writer who incorrectly translated 'oural' or 'ouran' – the Arabic name of a common African species – as 'waran' or 'warneidechse' meaning 'warning lizard'. This linguistic error gave rise to both the scientific name of the group Varanus and the English term 'monitor'.

There are about 44 living species of monitor lizard and not all of them are giants. The variation in mass among the species is nearly five orders of magnitude – about the same as the difference between a mouse and an elephant. Conservative in design, they are among the most streamlined lizards, unadorned by impressive frills and back spines or flamboyant bumps or horns. Their skin patterns can be colourful, particularly when young. The largest Australian species is also beautifully marked as an adult. This was the first species we filmed for *Giants*.

Australia has 27 kinds of monitor, the highest density of species occurs there. As many as six species co-exist together in the arid desert interior, and it also boasts the smallest monitor – the diminutive pygmy monitor with a total length of 2 m (6.5 ft) and a weight of 8–10 g (0.5 oz). The monitor we wanted to film, the perentie, can reach 2.5 m (8 ft) and weigh 15 kg (33 lb).

This magnificent reptile is found in rocky, arid regions and sand plains in all mainland Australian states except Victoria and it frequents many islands off the western coast. The film crew and I travelled to one of these, Barrow Island, which also happens to be one of my all time favourite places.

A jet chartered by an oil company to take their workers back and forth is one of the few ways to reach the sub-tropical island which is 1,300 km (808 miles) north of Perth. You would think this was an unpromising start for filming wildlife, but even though Barrow holds 9 per cent of Australia's oil reserves yielding about 14,000 barrels a day, it is also a Class A Nature Reserve and a place where industry and wildlife really do co-exist harmoniously. Only 4 per cent of

Barrow is affected by oil activities; once an operation is completed, West Australian Petroleum (WAPET) use earth moving machines to re-profile the area and replace the topsoil. Given enough time the land regenerates naturally.

Skimming the 234-sq. km (90-sq. mile) limestone island as we landed, it seemed to be covered with golden fields of skinny corn swaying in the wind, and studded with red termite mounds. Every now and then there was a beam pump, also known as a nodding donkey because of its shape and rhythmic up and down movements, for extracting the oil. Once we got close the corn fields were transformed into plains of spinifex, a prickly plant that grows in impenetrable hummocks. Nearly every plant had slender golden seed heads due to the recent rains. These plant fortresses provide a secure home for many of Barrow's 54 reptile species and 14 species of land mammal. The perentie is the largest terrestrial predator and the island's king. The lizards can be found anywhere on the island. Their lairs are usually in rock outcrops, and they can be seen in heraldic poses using termite mounds as a vantage point, walking along the dirt roads rather than battling through the spinifex and even amongst the pipes and metal works of the oil installations. Between December and March, however, they concentrate around the beaches because there is prey in the sand.

We were in position at 9 am the next morning. On sunny days activity would cease at 11 am or noon as temperatures could soar to 35°C (120°F). If it's too hot perenties sit out in the shade until the cool of the late afternoon. All of the beaches on the wave-cut west coast showed signs of intense monitor activity. Their

tails had gouged grooves in the sand, their size ensured every foot fall left a deep impression and their tracks criss-crossed the beach, often leading to and from craters in the sand.

These depressions held the prey they were looking for. Barrow's beaches are rookeries for green and flat-back turtles. The latter are unique to Australia, and breed nowhere else. During the nesting season perenties use their acute sense of smell to detect turtle eggs and hatchlings. All monitors have long, deeply-forked tongues which they frequently flick out to sample molecules in the air. The tips fit snugly into the Jacobsen's organs in the roof of their mouth. These chemical analysers are so sensitive that monitors can determine the direction of scents: if the concentration of odour is greater on the left tongue tip then the source will be on that side. The tongue tips are not far enough apart to make these directional readings totally effective, so to enhance them, many monitors swing their heads from side to side as they walk.

Despite the proliferation of perentie tracks, no lizards came to patrol any of the beaches we watched on that first day, and we had to content ourselves with filming a breakout of flat-back hatchlings. We caught the moment when they crept out of the sand before heading for the sea. This usually happens at night when there is less danger from sea gulls. Each nest may contain up to 100 hatchlings and all of them can be snapped up by the birds if they break out in daylight, so although I shouldn't really interfere, it is irresistible

Above, The perentie, one of 27 species of monitor lizard found in Australia, can reach 2.5 m (8 ft) and weigh 15 kg (33 lb). It is found in rocky, arid regions and sand plains in all mainland states, except Victoria, and also frequents many islands off the western coast

Right, As they head for the sea after breaking out, turtle hatchlings risk being preyed on not only by sea birds, but also the perenties, which can eat hundreds of the tiny creatures

Below, Russel Lagdon took this picture of a perentie that had caught and killed a female wallaroo. It took 45 minutes for the lizard to work the body into its mouth until just the hind legs and tail were visible

to collect up the babies and give them a helping hand to the water's edge. There are still sharks and other large fish, and even octopus for them to negotiate, but at least they are safe from aerial attack.

At night Barrow becomes a very special place indeed and you can see some of Australia's rarest and most endangered species. Relaxing with the oil men in the bar we were regaled with tales of giant perenties but this noisy exuberance didn't deter the local wildlife. A dropped peanut brought a rat-sized creature with a long pointed nose scurrying towards it. As it moved into the light its coat gleamed with the lustre of a precious metal. It was a golden bandicoot, which are common here but rare on the mainland; small populations are restricted to the remote Kimberley Mountains. The marsupial's tail lay along the edge of my shoe as it nonchalantly munched the nut, quivering its pointy nose. Grazing on the grass of the sports field there were other rarities; the size of small dogs, these animals hopped rather than ran – they were hare

wallabies. Burrowing bettongs are the last of Barrow's specialities. Slightly larger than the bandicoots, they look like miniature low-slung kangaroos with huge back legs, three-toed pink feet and black button eyes. Bettongs spend the day in complex warrens, hare wallabies fashion day beds out of spinifex, while the bandicoots favour hollows in termite mounds. These refuges provide shelter from the fierce sun as well as shielding them from perenties.

All these animals are potential prey for the lizards as is as Barrow's largest mammal, the wallaroo. These mammals have long, reddish hair and are somewhere between a wallaby and kangaroo in size, strong and stockily built. It seems unlikely that such a large animal can be caught and devoured by perenties but they can, at least when young. My friend Russel Lagdon, a WAPET's Environmental Officer, has witnessed this and has photographic evidence. Watching a perentie patrolling a rocky slope, he saw it startle a female wallaroo, almost a fully-grown joey. The predator sprinted at the fleeing mammals, pulling the smaller one down. Once the perentie's recurved teeth were anchored into the flesh of its prey, the wallaroo had no chance of escape. Violently shaking its head from side to side, the reptile smashed the joey against the rocks to kill it, before beginning the laborious process of swallowing the food down. Like snakes, monitors can digest large prey items as they have flexible connections between the bones in their skulls and an epiglottis that permits breathing even when their mouth is crammed with food. Even so, it was 45 minutes before most of the joey's body was inside the lizard's mouth and just the hind legs and tail hung outside.

A turtle's eggs or hatchlings are tiny compared to this enormous meal but perenties can eat hundreds of them. When digesting large meals perenties lie up in a rocky cleft or maybe a burrow. They excavate tunnels themselves, sometimes using a rodent burrow as a starting point, expanding and extending it until they have a burrow that could be 7–8 m (23–26 ft) long and 1 m (3 ft) below the ground.

We hoped that on our first visit our search had been fruitless because we had arrived between meals but that today a perentie would come to fill up. We decided to keep all our turtle eggs in one basket and concentrate on watching one beach. Between 9 am and 10.30 am we saw nothing but then at the far end of the beach, emerging from the marram grass, there was a

perentie on patrol.

We all sprinted towards the lizard so it didn't disappear into the vegetation. Unencumbered by heavy camera and sound equipment, I reached it first. It was big and beautiful. This individual was perhaps 2 m (6 ft) long; the maximum length of this species is 2.5 m (8 ft). It stood its ground tiliting its head to glare at me with a black and yellow eye set beneath an angular scaled brow. The long neck was exquisite, yellow above and white below, with a net-like pattern of black. The scales of the body made a pattern of smaller black and yellow reticulations, and superimposed on this were large gold spots edged with black, which increased in frequency along the whip-like tail.

The two Marks – Yates the cameraman and Roberts the sound man – and Bill Butt the director all caught up with me, so now I had to catch the perentie. The reptile swayed as I approached, its large neck pouch was distended and it expelled the air from this with a loud, rattling hiss. I jumped back as the reptile lashed out with its tail but I was too late, the stinging blow gave me a red weal on my leg. It has been reported that the tail lash of a perentie has smashed both the front legs of a dog.

Quickly I lunged at the tail, grabbing it firmly near the base. Now that defensive weapon was out of the equation, I still had to contend with the razor sharp teeth and formidable claws. A few years before I'd been bitten by a small perentie, a third of this one's size, and still have the scar. The teeth can tear into flesh with ease. As if to underline this the lizard threatened me

with an open mouth. Holding onto the tail with one hand I swiftly and surely grabbed the base of the neck with the other, gently pinning the lizard down as I did so. The purpose of all this was to film a direct impression of my height with the lizard's length but before I could lift it I needed to manoeuvre my hands to hold onto both pairs of legs as well as the neck and tail base. The well-muscled forelegs are used for digging up turtle nests and other prey, and these and the hind limbs have talon-like claws that can tear flesh and clothes to shreds.

There are even reports of monitors being used as living grappling irons. The lizard with a rope tied around its body is started up a wall. When the ascent is completed the man holding the rope gives a tug so the monitor digs its claws in, then the man pulls himself up the rope. Both warriors and burglars are reputed to have scaled buildings using this technique. Avoiding being snagged, I lifted the lizard aloft. It was at least as long as I was and probably weighed about 10 kg (22 lb). Perenties rarely weigh more than 15 kg (33 lb). I didn't have this load for long; as soon as Bill and Mark had achieved the shots they needed I gently put the perentie down and watched as it lumbered off along the beach. Well fed, its paunch barely cleared the sand. The lizard had obviously snaffled the contents of a turtle nest before I'd caught it, but the way it began to poke its head into craters in the sand, flickering its black tongue feverishly, made us believe it still had room for more.

Above, Lying next to the lizard Russel Lagdon and I could see how big and beautiful it was. Its long neck was yellow above and white below, with a net-like pattern of black. Superimposed on the pattern of black and yellow reticulations on its body and whip-like tail were large gold spots edged with black

Water Monitor

Australia may have the greatest diversity of monitors but the top three giants are all found in south-east Asia. One of them is occasionally found in swimming pools near my home in Bristol. The water monitor has the widest distribution of any monitor lizard, its range extending from Sri Lanka and the southern part of India, eastward to extreme southern China, the Phillipines and many of the islands of Indonesia.

All monitors need specialised conditions in captivity: spacious heated enclosures, a varied diet with vitamin and mineral supplementation as well as fluorescent lights that mimic, to some degree, natural sunlight. These things aren't to be taken lightly especially with water monitors that grow to such an enormous size – 2.7 m long (9 ft) and 61 kg (150 lb) in weight. If the right conditions are met, these lizards can become as tame as dogs. One that was 2.1 m (6 ft 11 in) long would snap instantly if proffered a dead rat, but ignore a human hand.

That's how I ended up in a swimming pool with one. 'Sally' had been acquired as a hatchling. (All monitors lay eggs, water monitors can lay up to 40 in a clutch.) Now ten years on he had outgrown the house of his carer and the *Giants* production team found a spacious new home for him in a reptile collection near London. This gave us a chance of filming a sequence of me taking him for a dip to show in one shot how he is longer than I am tall and how monitor lizards swim. Monty propelled himself with his tail in the manner of a crocodilian. He could dive and stay under water for at least 15 minutes. Monitors have been known to remain submerged for up to an hour. Amongst the great lizards, as their name suggests, water monitors are swimmers par excellence. They are never found far from this medium. Populations reach their heighest densities in mangroves, and their swimming prowess allows them to hunt for crabs, molluscs and other

aquatic food, as well as colonising small islands. They've been seen out in the ocean far from land. Sally had an endearing personality and to warm up after his swim he made an unusual if somewhat scaly and heavy scarf draped across my neck basking in the sun.

Water monitors seem adaptable and intelligent in the wild too. Cameraman Malcolm Ludgate, sound recordist Mark Roberts and I went to Tioman island to film them. Just off Malaysia's east coast, legend has it that this mystical island is the resting place of a magical dragon princess who, whilst flying from China to her beloved prince in Singapore, sought solace in the crystal clear waters of the South China Sea. So pleased was she with this idyllic spot she stopped there, foregoing her own happiness to give pleasure and comfort to fishermen and travellers by transforming into a beautiful island.

This delightful notion wasn't lost on us when we turned up at Salang, a village of stilted houses, to film reptiles. To me, these have always been real-life dragons, even though the mythical creatures were probably spawned in people's imaginations from encounters with crocodiles.

Large water monitors, many over 2 m (6 ft), were abundant there. Peering down from a rickety wooden bridge we could see them lazily swimming beneath us although this time I was glad I wasn't alongside, the water was the colour of coffee. Other monitors who weren't territorial lay indolently on the bank; medium ones lay spreadeagled over large ones so there were

piles of them in the dappled sunshine. An enormous one waddled past a couple of women working with palm fronds. After stripping off the leaves they'd bind the ribs of the fronds with rattan and make them into brushes for sweeping the floors of their houses. They took as much notice of the monitor as it did of them. They would have attracted his attention if they'd been discarding other rubbish that wasn't entirely plant material.

Only one monitor is primarily vegetarian – Gray's monitor of the Phillipines, which is mainly a fruit eater – all the rest eat animal matter whether it's dead or alive. Salang's water monitors grow so large by supplementing their natural diet of animals caught in the mangroves, by scavenging for any waste in the village. A café owner told us that the monitors had learnt that she threw out her food scraps at 5 pm and waited expectantly for these handouts. The village was also overrun with feral cats and there were probably rats too. If either of these mammals came within striking range they'd be swallowed with gusto. Water monitors will eat virtually anything including human

Left, Sally, our adopted water monitor, had an endearing personality. To warm up after her swim she made an unusual if somewhat scaly and heavy scarf draped across my neck

Below, The water monitor has the widest distribution of any monitor lizard. Its range extends from Sri Lanka and the southern part of India eastward to extreme southern China, the Phillipines and many of the islands of Indonesia

corpses. An eye witness account by an explorer late in the last century details how the Selung tribe of the Mergui archipelago leave their dead on a platform in the forest to be eaten up by monitors. He reports that in one of these grisly picnics up to 15 lizards were observed to take part. Until recently, tribes in Bali used monitors as undertakers too; corpses were put in baskets with a narrow opening that allowed lizards to enter but not monkeys.

Living in such close proximity to living people, the monitors in Salang village seemed as even-tempered as Sally, but not quite. If I sat still, they approached closely. We needed this to happen for the filming but on one occasion I made a sudden movement when I was a fraction too close. In a flash the monitor whipped its tail upwards almost over its back, lashing my head with the tip. I deserved this dressing down but to compound my indignity, Malcolm had great joy in telling me he'd caught it on film. At least it was a graphic illustration of how it isn't just perenties, but most great monitors, that use their tails in defence.

Crocodile Monitor

The longest lizard in the world is the magnificent and mysterious Salvadori's or crocodile monitor which has a tail that's at least twice, perhaps two-and-a-half times the length of its head and body. This makes a formidable whip and in captivity it has been reported to lash out at peoples' eyes with unerring accuracy. The tail's primary purpose is as a climbing aid for this largely arboreal species. When it is perched or moving along thin branches the tail acts as a counterbalance and it is prehensile too. On a tricky descent it can be coiled around branches to support the lizard's weight. As you'd expect with such a proficient climber, the toes have massive curved shiny black claws for clinging on and this species can even hang vertically holding on with its hind feet alone.

Strikingly coloured with scales of black and gold, this monitor gets the crocodile part of its name from its huge size and large bulbous snout. The longest reliably recorded was an astonishing 4.75 m (15 ft 7 in), but it is claimed that this species reaches 6 m (19 ft 8 in). The head of this creature is reminiscent of *Tyrannosaurus rex*. With reliance on smell the snout became more swollen and prominent with age, especially with old males. Why should this be so? As with many aspects of the crocodile monitor's natural history, sadly there is a paucity of information particularly in the wild.

The lizards are only found in Papua New Guinea, particularly the island's Indonesian territory of Irian Jaya. The remoteness of this region and the difficulty of observing this tree-living lizard in dense rainforest foliage is why it is still so enigmatic. Does it spend much time at the top of tall trees, is it only found lower down or can it be found at all heights? Does courtship happen above the ground or do pairs come down for this? Scientists are never sure.

It is known to take birds' eggs because one was found in the stomach of a preserved specimen, but does it do this routinely or only occasionally? It has a mouthful of sharp teeth so it surely hunts, but its relatively narrow and delicate jaws suggest the prey is likely to be small, perhaps birds and their chicks. Crocodile monitors are certainly not designed for overpowering large animals or swallowing down hunks of flesh as the world's biggest lizard does and even though they may be longer, their slight build means that they can't compete with the real giant amongst lizards in any reasonable assessment of size.

Right, The crocodile monitor is the longest lizard in the world. Strikingly coloured with scales of black and gold, it gets its name from its huge size and large bulbous snout. Sadly, information on the natural history of this species is very scarce

Komodo Dragon

Today Komodo dragons are the most famous lizards in the world but until recently this wasn't the case. There were rumours of giant lizards on the islands east of Bali and south of Borneo for as long as there were people there. Traders and fishermen brought back stories of a strange monster, the 'buaja darat' or land crocodile, but their veracity was not proved to the scientific world until 1912. Lieutenant van Steyn van Hensbroek, a member of a Dutch pearling fleet, killed a Komodo dragon in 1911. He sent a photograph and the skin of the 2.1 m (7 ft) reptile to the director of a museum in Java, Major P. A. Ouwens. He set about verifying the report sending an Indonesian collector to Komodo, who brought back the bodies of two adults measuring 3.1 m (10 ft) and 2.35 m (7 ft 9 in), as well as two live youngsters about 1 m (3 ft) long. Major Ouwens realised that the land crocodile was actually a monitor lizard. Now he had the honour of naming and describing a species that was new to science and he called it *Varanus komodoensis*.

Today we know these lizards are found on a few small islands in the Indonesian archipelago, which is incidentally, a giant itself. Made up of over 13,000 islands, it stretches for 5,200 km (3,230 miles) along the Equator. Komodo National Park is one of the few areas, perhaps the only area in the world, set aside specifically for a lizard. 1,700 dragons are found on Komodo itself; Rinca has 1,300, Gili Motang has about 100. Another 2,000 are found outside this protected area in the region of Flores, a much larger island.

I visited these spectacular animals with cameraman Jeff Goodman, soundman Mark Roberts and researcher Conrad Maufe. We left Bali to fly by jet to the island of Sumbawa. A ride in a rattling bus took us to the fishing port of Sape where we boarded our boat. Our first destination was the island of Rinca, a voyage of 15 hours.

Our first view was at sunrise. A mass of volcanic rock jutted into a watery blue sky. Scattered along the skyline were the silhouettes of lontar palms, the shape of exploding fireworks. As the sun rose higher more details were revealed; the flanks and plateaus of the island were covered in a tawny savannah. There were stripes and patches of monsoon forest too. These were as much brown as green, as many of the trees – tamarinds are one of the most common kinds – are leafless at this time of year. These islands are some of the driest areas in Indonesia. There are few permanent water sources and between March and November south-east trade winds from Australia give up little moisture. Our visit was in July. What little precipitation there is comes between December and February when the north-west monsoon comes from Asia. Although it deposits most of its rain over western Indonesia, it still provides enough moisture to sustain

Left, Found on a few small islands in the Indonesian archipelago, Komodo dragons are the most famous lizards in the world. The longest verified specimen measured over 3 m (10 ft) and in the wild they commonly weigh up to 70 kg (154 lb)

Above, Komodo Island, one of over 13,000 islands making up the Indonesian archipelago, is home to no fewer than 1,700 dragons

the patches of forest here.

We landed to explore all of these habitats because they can all hide dragons. First, we filmed water buffalo in the monsoon forest. By approaching silently and stealthily we got close to an old scarred bull drinking from a stream, one of Rinca's few permanent water sources. The dragons would wait in ambush next to game trails in the forest, launching a surprise attack when a buffalo or Rusa deer walked too close. The predator would attempt to smash its quarry to the ground before attempting to disembowel it with a slashing bite. The teeth of a Komodo dragon are awe-inspiring, reminiscent of a shark's. They are edged with hundreds of tiny serrations for sawing through flesh and hide.

More often than not, the prey is too large or powerful to be brought down, but a dragon's bite can be fatal on a different, longer time scale. The large serrated teeth harbour bits of flesh from the lizard's last meal. About 50 strains of bacteria, of which at least

seven are highly septic, have been shown to thrive on these fragments of flesh and the products of putrefaction that leak into the saliva, the net result being that an animal that has been bitten will probably die from septicaemia and other infections within a week. The body will then be devoured by dragons where it falls, although not necessarily by its original attacker, particularly if the wounded prey wanders far.

The deer and buffalo came to the island comparatively recently with people so there is speculation as to why Komodo dragons came to be giants. As a general rule reptiles will always have an advantage in a race to be top predators on tropical islands because they need little fuel and can survive long periods of fasting. These qualities are required on islands which have fewer resources than more substantial land masses.

Once the race to be a giant has been won, growing to a great size means that much larger prey can be taken, so no hunting opportunities are wasted. This still doesn't explain what the dragons preyed upon before man colonised the islands. There is scant fossil evidence but scientists believe that there were once pygmy elephants about 1.5 m (5 ft) at the shoulder on the dragon's islands. There wasn't enough food to support full-sized versions and the lizard's ancestors became large to be able to overpower them. When they became extinct the dragons could then easily make the switch to their modern day prey – deer, boar and water buffalo. Prey species similar to these may also have been present before the arrival of modern humans within the past 40,000 years.

On Rinca the smell of decay led us to the carcass of a water buffalo festooned with a dozen or so dragons. Their sense of smell is much more acute than mine so the odoriferous corpse could have attracted them from over 4 km (2.5 miles) away. They were of varying sizes, ranging from 1 m (3 ft) to 2.5 m (8 ft). The smaller ones circled the carcass and more especially the older dragons nervously; cannibalism is common. More brightly coloured than the dull grey or brown adults, the juveniles' scaly hides were patterned with orange and yellow. They showed the same signs of nervousness towards the larger dragons as the perentie had done to me on that beach in Australia, inflating the pouch under their throat with air and walking with an exaggerated swagger, perhaps to appear larger then they are.

The adults tore off hunks of flesh swallowing huge chunks at a time. Meals can be few and far between and eating quickly lessens the chance of another dragon stealing your meal. These monitors have moveable joints in their skulls, so their jaws can open wide, and expandable throats and stomachs to cope with large meals. The strong muscles in their jaws and throat help speed up the process of getting food inside them when they're bolting it down. They are capable of devouring 80 per cent of their body weight in a single sitting and a 42 kg (70 lb 8 oz) dragon was seen to consume a 30 kg (66 lb) boar in 17 minutes flat.

The carcass was badly decomposed but masses of seething maggots didn't put off the dragons one iota. After swallowing pieces of meat they licked their lips clean of wriggling fly larvae as if they were food experts dabbing a napkin on their mouths after a cordon bleu meal. During feeding the lizards may even sneeze to dislodge fly larvae from their nasal passages. Another large dragon buried his head into a dark recess of the corpse, pulling out a string of intestine which he

proceeded to shake violently, scattering the contents around him. This behaviour removes faeces from the meal. Even for some Komodo dragons, some things are unpalatable. Small Komodos have been observed rolling in faecal material. This odour shield puts off their larger brethren from eating them. One huge dragon managed to shake off one of the buffalo's forelegs which he swallowed whole, hooves and all. Large mammalian carnivores, lions for example, are wasteful, turning up their noses at intestine, hide, skeletons and hooves, usually leaving 25–30 per cent of their kill unconsumed. Komodos are more efficient diners leaving only about 12 per cent of a carcass.

Above, On the island of Rinca Komodo dragons often wait in ambush next to game trails in forests to launch surprise attacks on water buffalo. The predator tries to smash the beast to the ground before attempting to disembowel it with a slashing bite

We hoped to film courtship. May to August is the breeding season and you're most likely to observe it where there is a scrum of dragons around a food source.

Males of many of the larger monitor species indulge in ritualised combat when mature females are near. Standing almost vertically, using their tails as support, the two combatants embrace with their forelegs and begin to wrestle. Each one strains to throw the other to the ground. The loser will either lie still or run away, while the victor may have a chance of mating with the female if she hasn't already wandered off.

Unfortunately, this didn't happen around 'our' carcass but I wasn't disappointed. The feeding sequence was spectacular enough.

The female will lay her eggs in September. They have soft leathery shells and are each about 11 cm (4 in) long, the size of a swan's egg.

The clutch of about 50 are laid in soil depressions or in the abandoned or hijacked nest mounds of orange footed scrub fowl. These birds pile up heaps of soil and leaves that can be 3 m (10 ft) across and 1m (3 ft) high. This is the incubating medium for their own eggs which are warmed by the sun and the heat produced by fermentation of plant material. The compost also makes a perfect nursery for dragon eggs. These take about nine months to hatch but other than giving her clutch some protection by lying on the nest site for the

Left, Capable of devouring 80 per cent of their body weight in a single sitting, Komodo dragons have moveable joints in their skulls, so their jaws can open wide, and expandable throats and stomachs to cope with large meals

first three months, sometimes longer, female dragons show no maternal care when the young hatch.

The baby giants weigh less than 100 g (3.5 oz) and are about 40 cm (16 in) long. They are more strikingly marked than either adults or juveniles with a yellow green head, black stripes and bands on their neck and

Below, Komodo dragons have an acute sense of smell. The odoriferous, decaying carcass of a water buffalo can attract them from over 4 km (2.5 miles) away

Above, Unlike many large mammalian carnivores, which may leave up to 30 per cent of their kill unconsumed, Komodos are efficient diners, consuming almost the entire prey, including hooves, intestines and skeleton

forelegs and with lines of brick red circles along the length of their dark brown body. The dark brown tail is banded in dull yellow. Young Komodos face many perils such as birds of prey, snakes and older Komodos, so these lithe and agile lizards put themselves out of reach of larger, heavier members of their species by taking to the trees.

On a catholic diet of insects, geckos and other smaller lizards, snakes and even birds, they can grow to 2 m (6 ft 6 in) and attain a weight of 25 kg (55 lb) if they survive their first five years. From then on they are almost invincible and could be a dominant force on their tiny island kingdoms for 30 years or more.

I wanted to lie next to the largest dragon we could find and to do that meant a visit to the island of Komodo itself. The dragons there used to be fed for the tourists, a habit that has now been discontinued because the lizards were losing their natural instincts and becoming sluggish and obese. One famous dragon 'Ahwas', became huge by eating these handouts, and he can still be found around the camp where visitors stay.

We obtained special permission to bring a goat carcass to tempt him with. This would give me a chance to lie alongside him. It wasn't long before the aroma of

fresh meat brought Ahwas to us. He must be one of the world's greatest lizards. Within seconds he was trying to swallow the dead goat whole, a swallowing feat even he couldn't manage. As he was occupied, I lay down and Jeff filmed me stroking his head as he fed. You could never do this with a lion or tiger and most domestic dogs wouldn't even tolerate it. With truly wild Komodos it could be dangerous or more likely they'd be startled and run away. Ahwas is used to people and he didn't even bat his scaly eyelid. His length must approach that of the longest verified specimen, which was 3.13 m (10 ft 2 in) (females are smaller, about 2.5 m or 7 ft 6 in). He was certainly much longer than I am tall and with a stomach full of undigested food his weight could exceed 150 kg (331 lb), although a more typical weight for large wild dragons is 70 kg (154 lb). Ahwas shuffled his huge clawed foot and covered me in dust. I was right on the ground so when he swallowed a piece of flesh, lifting up his massive head, it towered above me. He looked me right in the eye and then his forked yellow tongue flickered out like a flame. It felt as if the tips brushed my face but I can't be sure. No human ever set eyes on a living dinosaur but surely this must be the next best thing.

Birds

From the largest flightless bird to the heaviest flying bird, to the bird with the greatest wing span, we travelled the world to find and capture all of these on film. Found in a variety of habitats these birds have developed remarkable methods of living, feeding, and breeding. Some of these birds were ugly, others were graceful, many were awe-inspiring, but they were all giants.

THE NOISE WAS DEAFENING. TO ACCELERATE WITH ENOUGH SPEED, THE CITROEN Diane car screamed along in second gear. To add to the commotion, I was calling at the top of my voice hoping against hope the experiment would work, the straight stretch of country lane would soon run out. The car's plastic roof had been rolled back and the cameraman and I stood where the back seats had once been. The driver tried to coax as much out of the engine as possible, but even though we'd picked up speed accelerating to 32 kph (20 mph), the brown shape was still ahead of us and too far away to film.

Suddenly with an imperceptible movement of its wings, the juvenile starling swerved in towards us materialising in the air space just above the driver's head. It was riding the bow wave of air made by the moving car just as dolphins use the bow wave of water made by ships in the ocean.

The bird was close enough to touch, so from right alongside, the cameraman could get shots of a starling in flight – the very first time this had been done. Wildlife camera team Des and Jen Butler had achieved it with snow geese, but to my knowledge nobody had tried this with a perching bird like a starling. I just watched, breathless with excitement, the film would always be a permanent record but there's nothing quite like being there, the warm June air speeding past my face, the tiny bird effortlessly hanging next to the car and the hedgerow of elderflower and hawthorn blurring into greens and whites.

At the end of that run, and we did many more after that, the starling did a tight circle and landed on my head. I'd hand reared it with three others since they were tiny chicks. I fed them on mealworms, chopped-up egg white and mincemeat sprinkled with vitamins, filling their ever-gaping orange maws every hour or so, from dawn until dusk. At first, I flew them behind the car one at a time, but eventually we could get film of the flock. When we'd finished filming they gradually gained their independence, although for three months afterwards, I could still impress the dog walkers in the park behind my house by whistling at a flock of wild starlings and having four of them peel away and land on my outstretched arm. One of the brood had a characteristic notch in its bill. I definitely saw that bird a year after they'd returned to the wild, so at least one of them had the skills for survival.

Flying with hand-reared birds, not literally of course, but having them fly alongside cars or speed-boats has given me some of the greatest thrills of my life. As well as starlings, I've been right next to all sorts of waterfowl, a sparrowhawk, even an owl but the most thrilling of all must be the whooper swans. For three years these swans have a juvenile plumage of dingy brown, and even their bills are pink and chocolate. Then, in the third autumn, they acquire snow-white feathers and a bill of bright yellow and matt black. I was unsure whether the bond to follow their rearers would be strong for that long but it was. They flew behind an open-top Citroen at an old air-field near Bristol and behind a speed-boat on a peaty lochan near Edinburgh. It was breathtaking to have two of these beautiful birds flying at 48 kph (30 mph), so close you could hear them drawing breath – sometimes they'd even gently pat you on the head with their wing tips. That close they seemed huge but they are medium-sized swans with a wingspan not exceeding 2.43 m (8 ft), a weight of 14 kg (31 lb). I knew both the trumpeter swans of North America and the mute swans, the birds that grace many of Europe's waterscapes, were larger, but I realised I didn't know for sure which are the giants amongst birds, or at least amongst those that can fly.

Right, The marabou stork has been described in many ways, most of them derogatory, but I have an affinity with these strange birds

Cassowary, Emu and Ostrich

I knew more about those that were permanently grounded. All of the really big flightless birds belong to the 'ratite' family. This name is derived from the Latin 'ratis' meaning 'raft' as these birds have a flat breastbone. Flying birds have a keel on theirs which provides extra anchorage for their large powerful flight muscles.

The big three ratites are cassowaries, emus and, of course, the ostrich. (South America's rhea and New Zealand's kiwis are in the group too.) There are three species of cassowaries – two species, the southern and single-wattled stand as tall as a man and weigh up to 65 kg (143 lb). The third, the dwarf cassowary, would only reach a man's waist and weighs only 25 kg (55 lb). I was in the habitat of the southern kind when I stayed at the aptly named 'Cassowary House' in Northern Queensland, Australia, a famous destination for bird-watchers. It is a haven for many rainforest species, white-tailed kingfishers, log runners and magnificent rifle birds to name a few, but for me the chance of a visitation by a cassowary was most thrilling of all.

Cassowaries are usually solitary, scouring the forest floor for fallen fruit, their main food. Laurel trees are particularly important – they produce fleshy fruits in spring and summer which are rich in protein and fat at the time of year the cassowaries nest. The birds' breeding success is very poor when the laurels fail to fruit, as they do every second or third year. So far, 21 species of rainforest plants have been found to be inextricably linked with cassowaries – they must pass through their digestive system to have any chance of germinating.

There's nothing predictable about a cassowary's walkabout – it depends on where the available fruit is. I was on the veranda of Cassowary House wrestling with the problematical identification of a honeyeater feeding on a banana on the bird table (was it a lewin's or yellow-naped? I couldn't decide), when there was a shout from the kitchen. There, standing in the green half-light under a dense canopy of leaves was a magnificent creature. He waited patiently for a hand-out of mangoes and bananas. For him, Cassowary House was a tree with guaranteed fruit at any time of year.

He moved one foot forward, his three toes splaying apart as they took his weight. Each toe had a strong claw to provide grip when running, the middle toe had a much longer, 12 cm (5 in), dagger-like spike. This is used in defence. People have been raked by these claws and even kicked to death by cassowaries protecting their young.

Sedately, the bird left the forest and approached a pile of over-ripe mangoes on the lawn. His black, glossy plumage shone with an oily lustre as he walked into the sunlight. His head and neck were as colourful as they were extraordinary. The naked skin had red lines down the sides of the neck, and a patch of orange at the back. The rest of it was blue, sky blue at the top, becoming darker at the base. About half-way up a pair of fleshy, bright red wattles swung from side to side as he gulped down the fruit. After eating he lifted his head. I'm about 1.9 m (6 ft) tall, the bird was 30 cm (1 ft) shorter.

I find it very difficult travelling through the rainforest to avoid low branches. You constantly have to stoop and duck, and if you try moving quickly you inevitably crack your head. For this eventuality, cassowaries have a crash helmet. The bony crest rose vertically from the pale blue skin on his head, the casque was grey in colour and pointed slightly forward. No other bird in the world has this type of protective armour.

This was a male bird because last summer the owners of the guest house said he was accompanied by stripy black-and-white chicks. In a single breeding season, females may mate and lay a clutch with two or even three different males, leaving all the parental duties to them. A male will incubate the pale green eggs. For two months after the young have hatched, he cares for them for another nine months or so.

Australia has even bigger flightless birds. They inhabit drier forests and the semi-arid plains of the continent's interior. They're so typically Australian, they even have a beer named after them. Of course, they're emus. They're the second largest bird in the world, standing some 150–190 cm (32–40 in) tall and weighing 35–55 kg (77–121 lb). Females are generally larger and heavier than males. Both sexes have a black head and neck, the feathers on the body are brown mottled with black.

Emus usually live alone or in pairs, although they may congregate in areas where water and food are abundant. Active by day, emus spend most of their time feeding, searching out the most nutritious parts of plants, seeds, fruits, flowers and tender roots; protein-packed caterpillars, beetles and grasshoppers are also on their menu. The birds have powerful three-toed feet and are marathon walkers. They can cover great distances at a steady 7 kph (4 mph), and if pushed they can sprint at 48 kph (30 mph), eating up 2.7 m (9 ft) of ground with every stride.

As with cassowaries, male emus take full responsibility for looking after the eggs and chicks. Incubation lasts around eight weeks. The males are extremely conscientious parents, warming and protecting the clutch of 5–15 eggs without eating, drinking or defecating. Their responsibilities continue for five months after hatching. The male will aggressively protect the chicks from dingos, foxes and people. At five months the young are half the size of an adult, but males remain with them for another two or three months; in exceptional cases they may remain for another year.

The ostrich, the world's largest bird, is also found in Australia, but it is a foreigner there. The population is made up of escapees from farms and ranches that have

Below, Native to Africa there are a number of different races of ostrich throughout the continent. Many are semi-wild having escaped from farms and ranches and successfully adapted to life on the plains, but there are wild populations in north Namibia, the Kalahari and possibly in south-west Angola. They are found on dry open plains and semi-desert

successfully adapted to life in the outback, a habitat not too dissimilar to the grasslands of Africa – their original home.

I had my first eyeball-to-eyeball meeting, and what an eyeball it was, at the Safari Ostrich Shaw Farm in Oudtshoorn, South Africa. The eyeball was twice the width of my own, 5 cm (2 in) across. In fact, it is the largest of any vertebrate on the land, even larger than that of an elephant. For me, to be at the same level with the ostrich, I had to stand on a box. Its long stout legs and periscope neck hoisted its head 2.5 m (8 ft) above the ground – as tall as the crossbar in a football goal. Being tennis-ball sized wasn't all the eyes had to commend them. A deep, liquid brown, they were fringed by elegant black lashes that a Hollywood starlet would die for. The bird looked at me with indifference. There was no hint of animosity which I hoped wouldn't change when I clambered on his back – irate ostriches have shattered a man's skull with a single kick.

There was no saddle. I had to perch precariously on the bony back with my thighs under the stubby wings and my legs braced against the tops of the bird's legs. I held on to the wings. The feathers were the most unusual I'd ever felt. The ostrich, like all ratites, doesn't have hooks on the barbs of its feathers, so they don't zip together to give the firm, flat surface of the feathers of other birds. Instead they are loose – the overall feel was really soft and smooth.

The race I was in would last no longer than six seconds. On either side of me there was another trained ostrich, each with an experienced rider. This was my

first time. With a shout, we were off. I had to keep my legs locked tightly to restrict the movement of my steed's legs. Ostriches are fantastic runners, they can cover 50 kph (41 mph) in just 30 minutes, or sprint at 70 kph (43 mph). This means they could outrun a racehorse, or complete the London Marathon in 39 minutes. It would also mean if my piebald ride was going full speed, I'd fall off in a second. I managed to hold on and even notice the puffs of sand coming up from the feet of other ostriches. They're the only bird in the world with two toes. This lessens the surface area exposed to the ground – cutting down friction helps ostriches to be the fastest creatures on two legs. By keeping my legs locked to make the ostrich take slightly shorter strides than the 3.5 m (11 ft) ones it would take at full pelt, and by leaning back as far as I could, I was rather proud to complete the course even though I was last.

My exhilarating ride showed me one of the many advantages that ostriches gain by being giants. When aboard and sitting upright, my head was the same height as the ostriches. I was on a moving observation tower. I could see a long way but couldn't imagine the scope of the ostrich's vista. If I had his keen eyesight, I could make out objects 3.5 km (2 miles) away. This is crucial on the African plains where predators abound. The birds make this early warning system even more effective by living in groups which maintain contact even when they are sleeping. If you watch a group at night, some will be sitting down with their necks raised. Their eyes are shut, but they're only sleeping lightly, and are still alert. Others stretch their necks out on the ground in front of them. They're in a deep sleep. Throughout the night the birds indulging in each type of rest chop and change. In this way there is little chance of nocturnal hunters springing a surprise.

Foraging in a group means there are more pairs of eyes to look out for predators. Ostriches feed mainly on vegetable matter. They are entertaining to watch when they're cramming in a mass of leaves. The skin of their neck stretches as the gobbet of food makes the long journey down their neck. Again, their large size brings them advantages. They can stretch for food out of reach of most plains antelope, and inside their bodies they have room for giant intestines 14 m (46 ft) long. They also have a gizzard filled with pebbles and stones which they've swallowed. This is an effective grinding mill for hard-to-digest leaves and grasses.

The male bird I'd ridden was as black as oil, with

white wings and tail. Females have brown bodies; the rest of their feathers are dirty white. Ostriches have 16 primary feathers on their stubby wings which the male uses to enhance his courtship display. In a bizarre dance, he rhythmically shakes his left wing, beating it against the side of his body, then he switches wings and beats the opposite flank. At the same time he sways his bright pink neck which is inflated with air. His tail is pumped up and down providing the dance's vertical component. His pink penis (male ostriches are in a select company with waterfowl – few birds have them at all) is also shown off during courtship. He'll be able to use it to mate with more than one female if his territory, which could be anything from 2–14 sq. km (1–5 sq. miles), is a good one. In marginal areas ostriches are monogamous.

If a male does have a harem, he and the 'major' hen take it in turns to incubate the eggs; the more conspicuous male looks after them at night. If a brooding bird is frightened, it may stretch its head out in front hoping it won't be noticed. This is how the old wives tale of an ostrich burying its heads in the sand may have come about. The 'major' hen is the male bird's main female but he will mate with up to 18 'minor' hens as well. Each of them lays an egg every two days for about a fortnight. The nest is 3 m (10 ft) across, but it needs to be that large. One nest near Nairobi contained 78 eggs. Each egg, the largest laid by any bird, is 160 mm (6 in) long, 31 mm (1 in) wide, with a shell 2 mm thick; incubating ostriches can get up to 25 eggs underneath them. Remarkably the 'major' hen can recognise her own eggs by size, weight or perhaps the arrangement of the pores in the shell. She arranges her clutch in the centre of the nest, surrounding them with an edible moat of sacrificial eggs, laid by the 'minor' hens, which are the

first to be taken by the marauding jackals, vultures, lions or hunting dogs. This arrangement is good for both the 'major' and 'minor' hens. The former has expendable eggs to help protect her own, the latter have a chance of getting their eggs hatched without taking the time and ensuing risks of incubation.

In about seven weeks, the eggs hatch. Within three days, the chicks can run and they're half the weight of the adults in just five months. Sometimes, there's an amazing sight on the savannah, a pair of adult ostriches with an entourage of 100–300 chicks. The peculiar habit of kidnapping the broods of others means that successful kidnappers may have a super brood. Ostriches mature after three or four years and can live for 25–35 years after that. The big three ratites are truly gigantic but for me, what makes a bird a bird is its power of flight. So what are the biggest ones that can lift off the ground?

Above, *left and right* During the race if I'd let my ostrich go at his natural speed I'd have fallen off in a second. I managed to finish even though I came last. It lasted just six seconds *Below*, It is no surprise that the world's largest bird lays the largest eggs

Marabou Stork

A contender for the flying bird with the greatest wing span is also found in Africa. There are authentic records of 2.63 m (8.5 ft) to 2.87 m (9.5 ft), and Colonel Meinertzhagen, a good naturalist and usually a reliable observer of a specimen, claimed to have shot one in 1934, which he estimated to be 4.06 m (13 ft 4 in) from wing tip to wing tip. If this had been authenticated this would be a record for any bird found over land or sea.

There's one place where, between 9 am and 6.30 pm, not five minutes goes by without the shadow of one of these giant birds passing over you. That place is Kampala, the capital of Uganda, and the birds sailing above it are marabou storks. I first really appreciated their majesty from a thirteenth-floor balcony in the Sheraton Hotel. Some of the storks were below me, some at eye level. I watched others sail upwards on their broad, long wings until they disappeared from sight, reaching an altitude of perhaps 4,000 m (13,000 ft). Most of the birds I could look down on were a dark black with a ladder of white along the middle of their wings (the secondary covert feathers are this colour). If they came close enough and the light was just right there was a green gloss to their flight feathers, and their back and mantle had a blue sheen. A few individuals still had the ladder of white feathers but they were dove grey above. These birds were in breeding plumage but were in a minority as it was February, the tail end of the breeding season in Uganda. All of the birds had massive pink bills and lots of bare skin on their head and necks. The colour of this was variable too, blackish red with a patch of bright blue on the back of the neck. They all looked like they'd been in the sun for many years, and patches of black pigment brought to mind the worst possible liver spots.

Some of the birds climbed past and then above me, so I could see their white feathers underneath their bodies, with an extension onto their pitch black wings. Some of the longer, fluffy feathers rippling in the breeze were the ones that once caused them to be very

Left, Marabous have massive bills and lots of bare skin on their head and necks. Colours are variable but mostly blackish red with a patch of bright blue on the back of the neck. They all looked like they'd been in the sun for many years, and patches of black pigment made me think of age spots

Below, Kampala, Uganda was where we came to see the extraordinary marabou stork. These huge birds co-habit quite contentedly with the human population in this busy capital city. The trees that lined the streets were inhabited by breeding birds and they also maintained sentry duty on the top of lamp posts

rare birds indeed. These feathers were much sought after by the millinery trade – the marabou down of their most expensive hats – so many of the birds were shot. The real explanation for this type of feather is thought to be to do with keeping cool. It also seemed that they had all stood in a very deep tin of shiny, white emulsion. Marabous actually have black legs but when they defecate – you've guessed it – they spray paint their legs with guano to reflect the fierce heat of the equatorial sun.

The best place for ground level views of marabous is at the abbatoir. To get there we drove down Nile Avenue, one of this busy city's main thoroughfares, past Uganda's many-windowed parliament house, so reminiscent of a giant dovecote. The road was lined with ornamental trees which were both beautiful and bizarre, beautiful because they were festooned with blossoms of delicate lilac, and bizarre because any that were strong enough cradled the nests of marabous. Each one contained 1–2 chicks, either fluffy and white, hatched about a month before, or larger young already with the black-and-white plumage of the adults. Some of the fledglings flapped their wings vigorously, hovering a few inches above the nest, a feat they can achieve aged about two months. At three months they are able to make short flights.

The trees needed to be strong to take the weight of stick nests, 30 cm (1 ft) deep, nearly 1 m (3 ft) across; some were nearly completely thatched. Four or five stork nests left the trees little room in their crown for leaves. The boughs must also be able to absorb the shock of the returning 9 kg (19 lb) adult birds that are certainly not light on their feet. For once I was pleased that the traffic was moving slowly as an adult marabou swooped over us, 'back flapping' to lose speed and brought itself to a standstill at its nest.

Only when they are younger than 30 days old do chicks need a parent constantly at the nest. To meet their demands the parents take it in turns to shade the nest with their wings and to find food. After they reach 30 days old, the chicks can be left alone and given more substantial meals, three times or maybe just twice a day The adult I'd just seen land did a most surprising thing. Shaking violently as if about to be sick, the bird regurgitated a watery cascade, dousing the chicks to cool them. He'd gathered the water from a nearby pond and dumped it at the nest, reminding me of the water-carrying planes that are used to fight forest fires.

Further down the road, other storks were loafing on

the top of lamp standards. One sat with its legs doubled up underneath as if it was kneeling, but in reality it wasn't his leg at all. In all birds, the part we think of as the leg is, in fact, the bare tarsus, technically part of the foot. Another stretched out its left wing just as a stream of cars below it turned in that direction, as if it was a policeman directing the traffic, a coincidence of course. Kampala residents hardly take any notice of giant birds loafing about in their city, new visitors are an exception. When she first arrived, one lady wondered which sculptor was responsible for the delightful bird statuettes decorating the top of the street lamps, until one of them launched itself pterodactyl-like into the air.

At the abattoir there were marabous on the ground, in serried ranks along every paddock fence and roof, with many more circling above. The cattle being slaughtered here are Ankoles, the African kind with huge, swept-back horns. I approached a group of marabous bickering and squabbling over a huge pile of these horns; presumably there were meaty scraps still attached. Crouching low, the birds seemed gigantic; they stand 120 cm (4 ft) tall. Hitchcock's film 'The Birds' would have been all the more terrifying had these been 'the birds' that attacked. The marabou has been variously described as 'the world's ugliest bird', 'a dirty old man with a skin disease of scalp', 'a creature stiff-jointed and dried up as if it has lived for 100 years' (the average life-span for a marabou is a quarter of this). I think this is unfair. I've always loved nature's oddities and marabous are certainly one of those. They are scruffy and gangling but on an old school report, my headmaster wrote precisely that about me – perhaps that's one of the reasons I have an affinity with marabous.

Marabous are designed for cleaning up. A mustering is a delightful collective noun for a group of these birds. Their work is taken for granted, but without their efforts, the abattoir would be knee-deep in offal. They also scrounge from Kampala's skips and bins. If they had fully-feathered heads and necks, they would soon become matted and filthy with congealed food.

They have a remarkable system of air sacs. On their neck there is the gular pouch – this was the fleshy protuberance I'd seen hanging from one of the storks in flight. It can be inflated at will to spectacular effect, giving a reddy pinkish or pink magenta sausage of nearly naked skin, which hangs 30 cm (1 ft) or more from the front of the neck. To us, a distended gular

pouch may look ridiculous, even slightly rude, but for other marabous it means 'I'm a top bird, keep out of my way'. Only dominant individuals display them. There's another element of the air sac system that is even more bizarre. It is bright red and situated on the back of the bird's neck – it reminds me of a blow up plastic strawberry. This is inflated if a marabou is feeling apprehensive and nervous.

If you can cope with the atrocious smell at Kampala's abattoir, you can watch the stork's behaviour at close range. During filming, the birds approached until they were barely 1 m (3 ft) away. By looking at the various degrees of inflation of their sacs as they bickered and squabbled, I could work out a rough pecking order, a very apt phrase for these birds. Their formidable bills grow continuously throughout their lives and can exceed 30 cm (1 ft) in length. Their beaks look menacing but the marabous don't use them to kill large living animals, and they are not particularly good for dismembering carcasses. This is why marabous in the natural state must wait for hyenas and vultures to tear open carcasses before nipping in to snatch morsels dropped by other scavengers. The morsels they can cope with can be quite large. With their elastic throats they can swallow chunks of food weighing up to 1 kg (2 lb). The abattoir's pre-sliced offal is perfect for them.

Marabous feed in all sorts of other ways and situations too. Few African fishing villages are without an entourage of these storks, ever vigilant for fish that

Above, The marabou's nests are 30 cm (1 ft) deep and almost 1 m (3 ft) across; some were nearly completely thatched. For the first 30 days of their lives the chicks need constant attention; the parents take it in turns to shade the nest with their wings and to find food. After they reach 30 days old, the chicks can be left alone and given more substantial meals, three times or maybe just twice a day

Right, Marabou storks have a remarkable system of air sacs. Hanging from the neck is the gular pouch which can be inflated at will to spectacular effect producing a reddy-pinkish or pink-magenta sausage of nearly-naked skin, this hangs down 30 cm (1 ft) or more

Below, The marabou's beaks look menacing but they are not used to kill large living animals, and are not even very good for dismembering carcasses. This is why marabous in the wild snatch morsels dropped by other scavengers. The abattoir's pre-sliced offal is perfect for them

have fallen out of the nets, or titbits from when the catch is cleaned. If fish become highly concentrated, marabous will catch their own, wading through drying pools with their submerged beaks half open. When a fish swims into the gap they snap their mandibles shut. Opportunistic predators, they'll also make aerial sorties to trawl for swarming termites, swallow the chicks or eggs of qualea finches, nest and all, and even stab, then drown, adult flamingos, causing whole breeding colonies to desert if their attacks become persistent.

Scavenging is what marabous are best at, and I hope there's always offal for them at Kampala's abattoir. Hopefully, their nests will never be tidied away from the tree-lined streets. Like magpies in Europe's urban centres, they're a breath of the wild in the city. The marabous save their greatest extravaganza for 1 pm every day. By then the business of butchering at the abattoir is over and there are no more hand-outs. The marabous seem to know this, and the giant birds face into the breeze in unison, then bounce and hop into the air. I could hear their splayed primaries creaking and squeaking as they took off, then they were gone.

Andean Condor

In South America there's another contender for the title of biggest-winged land bird, the Andean condor. But it isn't just size that links them to marabous even though they seem to be totally different types of birds. Recent genetic studies have shown that the New World vultures (Andean condors are the largest birds in this group), are related to storks. There are also long-legged fossil vultures so it is possible that these were the ancestors of modern-day storks.

I first saw Andean condors in a place befitting this majestic giant: the Colca Canyon in Peru, a huge cleft in the earth's crust that stretches for over 100 km (62 miles), and is twice the depth of Arizona's grand canyon. Looking over the edge of this huge void, there are no railings between you and the sparkling river at the bottom, 3,000 m (9,800 ft) below. This, combined with the effects of altitude, gives a truly heady effect. In this slightly unsteady state, I suddenly heard a whoosh – the unnaturally clear air seemed to magnify the sound – as the Andean condor swept past. Pink-headed with a collar of fluffy white down, the rest of the Condor's feathers were completely black, except for white panelling on its enormous wings.

The condor came so close I felt I could almost reach out and touch it. Until it cleared the sun's disc the bird shaded my face and the bright light was just visible through the tops of its wings. Soon it was out of sight. Condors can float to an altitude of 8,000 m (26,000 ft), jet liners usually fly at 10,000 m (33,000 ft). Another ten condors lifted out of the gorge, before the air show was over. This is an outstanding place to see the world's most perfectly-adapted soaring bird. With massive wings 3.2 m (10 ft) across (the other rarer species of condor, the Californian has a smaller wingspan of 2.7 m (9 ft)) condors can afford to have huge bodies weighing up to 15 kg (33 lb).

Of the ten birds I saw, six were males adorned with a comb of vivid pink skin on their heads, and pink wattles hanging from their necks. One bird whooshed so close, I could see the colour of its eyes – the iris was a yellowish brown. The females were smaller, with a reddish iris, and lacked the comb and wattles. All of the birds were accomplished fliers. As they shot over the lip of the canyon, an area of thermal turbulence, they folded the fingers of their wing tips for more control. Once in a smoother air flow, their primary feathers splayed apart to give the greatest area for gliding once more. They seemed to be soaring very purposefully and recent studies with vultures have shown that they may have an internal map of thermals, being able to memorise and recognise points in the landscape that provide the best uplifts of air.

Rising currents of air and the ability to find them are crucial to birds such as these. Colca Canyon is in the Andes, and mountainous regions or sea cliffs have rock walls which deflect the wind skywards to hold gliding birds aloft. Giant soaring birds are also found over plains and deserts. Here they rely on thermal upcurrents to sustain soaring flight. The sun warms the air above bare ground until it is hot enough to break away from the surrounding air mass. That's why vultures are forced to be late risers. The condors rose out of Colca Canyon at 10 am – the bubbles of light, warm air that carry them through the atmosphere are only there in the heat of the day. Once airborne, they rise higher and higher until something catches their attention, then they break away and glide slowly to another source of rising air.

This method of flight is probably why both condors and marabou storks have giant wings. With these and energy from rising air, flight is almost effortless. Low travel costs means they can cover more ground and find

more carrion which is widely dispersed. Once they were high above the canyon, the condors I'd watched would use their superb eyesight to scan the mountain slopes for the body of a vicuna that had perished in an avalanche or a cow that had died unseen by a rancher. Sky-hopping between thermals they'd lose altitude, gliding ever closer. The large white panels on their upper wings were conspicuous from afar and a signal to others that there's a feast in the offing.

The first birds to arrive would use their powerful bills to tear through skin to extract the muscle and viscera from the carcass. After bolting down up to 2 kg (4 lb) of food, two-thirds of their body weight, the bright yellow skin of their crop would bulge, a signal to others that they'd have their fill. Late arrivals would squabble for any scraps. In the past, one could see up to 40 birds at a carcass but now this is a rare spectacle.

Condors have always been important to people of the Andes, incorporated on pottery designs, textiles and carvings of pre-Columbia cultures. Gigantic representations of condors are part of the huge designs drawn by civilisations 1,000–2,000 years ago on the Nazca Plain in Peru. The ancient Incas of Peru thought condors were a special divinity carrying the sun

Above, The Andean condor has huge wings measuring 3.2 m (10 ft) across. These enable them to support their 15 kg (33 lb) bodies while flying. They can reach an altitude of 8,000 m (26,000 ft). The fingers of their wingtips are used to give extra control while flying in turbulent air

skywards each morning, messengers to the Gods. Today, although some are shot by ranchers because they think they attack livestock (in fact, the birds are too slow and their talons too blunt and weak to really do this), condors are still respected by most Andean people.

From Colonial times to the present day, the condor has played a pivotal role in a bizarre ritual. The Yawa Festival, 'Festival of Blood', takes place in the high Andean villages around Cuzco in Peru. I observed the sad spectacle in 1999. Rushing through a band of revellers, whose drunken attempts to play the local instrument, a trumpet called the waka woqa, were tuneless to say the least, I joined another noisy throng on top of a wall at the perimeter of a grassy plaza. Inside, the fiesta was coming to a climax. The excited crowd whooped as the tormented bull whirled around. It was tormented because there was a condor tied to its back. The bird was full-sized but its dingy brown plumage told me it was a juvenile. Wings outstretched, it fought for balance, its claws scrabbling for a purchase on the enraged bull's back. As if they were matadors, young men waved their jackets, jumping in the path of the petrified animals, sometimes goading the bull even more by spitting beer into its nostrils. The blood that gives the festival its name came from these youths. The ordeal is cruel for the bird and bull but they are usually unharmed. The only blood I saw spilled came from a village boy pricked by the bull's horns and another who had collided with the wall of the bullring as he escaped a charge. Their injuries weren't serious, and after an hour or so, this sad spectacle was over.

The Yawa Fiesta is symbolic in two ways. It happens on 28 July, the anniversary of Peru's liberation from Spanish rule. The bull and the condor symbolise the conflict between the conquistadors and the native Indians. The condor, battered and frightened but always uninjured, represents the successful resistance of the Indians. For some it is also a fertility rite, the blood is an offering to Pacha Mama ('Mother Earth'), a plea for the rains to come.

The next day the condor was released back into the Andean skies; even though its ordeal must have been terrible, at least it would be okay and, most importantly, no condors in that region are ever hunted, because of the people's reverence for them. Four days earlier, it had been attracted to bait, the carcass of a horse. After feasting on flesh it had become so bloated it couldn't take off, so was relatively easy to catch. For now the Peruvian government still grants a licence for capturing a condor but soon public opinion may see this tradition outlawed. It may even become impossible because of a scarcity of condors. Found throughout the Andes cordillera, from Tierra del Fuego to southern Colombia, their habitat is shrinking. The birds are part of the coat of arms of Colombia, Bolivia, Chile and Ecuador. In Ecuador, where they are the national bird, only 70 remain, and 31 of those are in captivity. All over their range a severe reduction in freely-available carcasses has brought about their decline. Old horses are no longer released to die and become condor fodder, land reforms have meant that smaller farms have replaced most large ranches, meaning fewer cattle. Ironically condors even lose out in national protected areas because livestock are excluded and there's no food for them. In the modern world there's not enough room for these carrion eaters which need large territories to find enough carcasses. I hope their fate is not the same as the Californian condor, a bird on the verge of extinction.

Left, The condor's sharp eyes scan the ground from the air in search of dead animals. The iris of the male's eye is yellowish-brown while the female's is reddish. The male bird had a comb of vivid pink skin on its head and a pink wattle hanging from its neck; the female has neither. A lack of freely-available carrion has brought about the decline of this species throughout their range. In Ecuador, where the condor is the national bird, only 70 remain

Albatross

The wingspan of condors and marabous is exceeded by birds that soar over the sea. They are beaten by both the wandering and royal albatrosses. From Australia there's an authenticated record of a wandering albatross measuring 3.6 m (12 ft) from wing tip to wing tip. Royals are about the same size. There are 12 species of albatross in all, but the two next largest, the shy of the Southern Ocean and the waved of the Galapagos Islands, have wingspans of 2.5 m (8 ft) and 2.3 m (7.5 ft) respectively, a long way behind the two species of giant albatross.

It was in Australia that I first saw these charismatic birds. For nearly half a century a research group has been meticulously recording individuals and a unique population. A study was begun in the 1950s, by Alan Setter and Doug Gibson. By ringing birds, they discovered that wandering albatrosses return to the same stretch of ocean near Wollongong, a town 75 km (47 miles) south of Sydney, every year. In fact, it is the only place in the world where wandering albatrosses from different breeding colonies meet up year after year. That patch of sea still has albatrosses today and the work is continued by Harry Batton, Lindsay Smith and Janice Jenkins of the Southern Oceans Seabird Study Group (SOSSA).

A film crew and I joined them on a small fishing trawler on a perfect sunny day. However, just because we were in Australia below a flawless blue sky didn't mean it was warm. As the boat left the harbour, I put on a sweater, fleece and windproof jacket. July is midwinter in the southern hemisphere. Even close inshore, the sea wasn't flat calm, and by the time we were 32 km (20 miles) out, the horizon seemed to rise and fall as we rode a swell half the height of a house. For the albatrosses though, this latitude of 34° was almost a

tropical holiday compared to the gales and heavy seas in the roaring '40s and furious '50s where they are usually found.

Now 'chumming' could begin, a delightful word describing a procedure that's far from delightful. Lindsay stirred a foul-smelling liquid full of fish heads and offal and bucketfuls of this stuff was then tipped over the side. An oily slick was left in our wake, a sort of floating bird table for sea birds.

Before long, nearly clipping the tops of the waves, petrels glided in on stiff wings. Gull-sized and cigar-coloured, they rose up as if being pulled short by an invisible tether, their way of braking before dropping down to snatch a floating morsel of fish. Then out of the corner of my eye, blue-grey shapes flickered into view; these much smaller birds were fairy prions. They moved so fast it was difficult to see them in detail, but they all had a broad black 'M' across their lower back.

Both the prions and petrels are tube-noses. This name comes from the pair of raised tubes on the tops of their beaks. They usually have a runny nose as the birds drink seawater, draining excess salt through their nostrils. The tube-nose may also be used to gauge air speed and to detect odours. Many of these birds have an acute sense of smell to locate food in the vastness of

Above, The wandering albatross is master of flight. They exploit the interaction of wind and water so well that they are able to fly just above the waves. Perfectly designed for gliding, a technique known as 'dynamic soaring' allows albatrosses to fly considerable distances without flapping their wings. These huge birds weigh around just 7 kg (15 lb)

the ocean and that is how some of them find slicks from chumming. Some may even locate their nest sites by scent.

As the providence petrels squabbled for scraps, one of the largest members of the tube-nosed group swept towards us. It had to be one of the giant species of albatross. Even though it was quite far away it looked huge. Its body was white but as it banked I could see there was a triangular wedge of white feathers extending onto each black wing, The wings of both wandering and royal albatrosses lighten with age, a process that takes about 20 years. The wings of the wanderer whiten from a central patch. If I'd been watching a royal albatross, whitening would start from the wing's leading edge.

Effortlessly it cut down the distance between us without a single wing beat. The giant achieved this gravity-defying feat by a technique called 'dynamic soaring'. Condors and marabous use their great wings to harness the energy from updrafts but out in the ocean, even though there are updrafts on the windward side of waves, they are not powerful enough to maintain height. In the ocean there's another property of the wind which albatrosses use to glide. The sea's surface slows wind down by friction so that wind speed at sea

level could be half of what it would be 20–30 m (60–100 ft) above the wave crests. Albatrosses exploit this property to glide along a course by swooping, wave skimming and climbing. The wind was in my face and sometimes the bird came straight towards the boat. Then with a flick of its great wings, it turned into the wind, swooping down into the layers of lighter wind at the sea's surface. As it dropped you could see the momentum from its weight speed it up. The albatross converted this speed and any updraft from the waves to lift, looping back on course. By this method, it had come closer to the boat but still maintained its height. The albatross could gauge the interplay of wave and wind so expertly, it would sometimes disappear behind a wall of blue water before materialising again above a wave crest, manoeuvring with such precision that a wingtip would sometimes actually touch a wave.

These birds have a giant wing span because there is no land in the storm-tossed southern ocean (a broad corridor ten times the area of the United States which completely encircles the globe between Antarctica and the other continents) to dissipate the strength of the wind. They have room to wander and their flight is virtually free. Wind power provides 98 per cent of the energy they need to fly.

Albatrosses really are sea birds par excellence, spending 80 per cent of their life over the ocean. They only require land to nest, incubate eggs and rear young. This wanderer would have spent years at a time roaming the southern oceans. Birds don't breed until their tenth or twelfth year, and so until then they've no need for terra firma.

The birds that spend the southern hemisphere winter at Wollongong, nest on tiny remote islands in South Georgia, the Crozets, Macquarie and several others. They're attracted to this particular stretch of ocean off Wollongong by another giant. Our boat was floating above the breeding grounds of giant cuttlefish. Like salmon, vast numbers of them die after spawning, and their bodies provide a feast for scavenging birds. Albatrosses don't just feed on carrion, the larger ones hunt octopus, squid and fish.

The wanderer reached us, alighting on the sea at the back of the trawler; this bird knew about leftovers from fishing boats. As Lindsay and Janice threw offal and fish scraps into the sea, it lunged at the food using its huge pink bill as forceps. Tipping back its head, it took nearly 30 seconds to swallow a fish head.

Now came the difficult part, Lindsay had to catch it. He leaned further over the sea as the bird edged closer, tempted by fish scraps. Suddenly Lindsay grabbed it, the struggling albatross was hauled aboard. He gently put his arm around the goose-sized body and clamped the beak shut with his hand. This is important as the bill can, quite easily, snip off a finger. The wanderer's vital statistics were put on record quickly. Lindsay and Janice examined and measured, assessing the bird's moult and plumage state, as well as noting whether it had any parasites such as feather lice. I helped to find out its measurements. Its beak was 10 cm (4 in) long, and it had a wingspan of 2.85 m (9 ft 4 in); its long wings seemed to fold in the most unlikely places as they ended up back against the body. Finally Janice

Above, The wandering albatross is master of flight. They exploit the interaction of wind and water so well that they are able to fly just above the waves. Perfectly designed for gliding, a technique known as 'dynamic soaring' allows albatrosses to fly considerable distances without flapping their wings. These huge birds weigh around just 7 kg (15 lb)

simple way to keep them away during the critical few seconds between the tossing out and sinking of the baited hook. All that is needed is a long, coloured streamer behind the back of the boat which crackles in the wind. That's enough to scare the albatrosses away. If this device was used on every long-line fishing boat, the accidental catching of wanderers would stop.

I was given the honour of releasing our newly banded albatross. I gently cradled my hands beneath it and lifted it up for launch. We knew it weighed 7.2 kg (15 lb 13 oz) precisely – for a giant it felt lightweight. Albatrosses are perfectly designed for gliding. No other bird even gets near their fixed wing flying ability. In all the best gliders wherever weight can be saved it has been. I lifted my arms and the bird's huge wings unfolded taking it over the rimless ocean, once more.

Below, It was a cold July day (mid-winter in the southern hemisphere) when I set out with the team from the Southern Ocean's Seabird Study Group. We managed to catch this wandering albatross and haul it on board so that we could measure and band it. The bird's beak alone measured 10 cm (4 in) and its wingspan was 2.85 m (9 ft 4 in)

fitted a numbered band onto its leg. The banding studies that started so many years ago have given clues that numbers of wandering albatross are declining. In the 1980s, several hundred were seen in a season. Today you're lucky to see a dozen.

Long-line fishing is the probable cause. Fishermen use huge lines up to 100 km (62 miles) long with baited hooks spaced every few metres to catch tuna. As the lines are paid out, if wanderers can get the bait, they're doomed. They swallow the hook and are dragged under by the line. Hundreds, maybe thousands of wandering albatrosses are drowned this way every year – a terrible toll when there are only 20,000 breeding pairs in the world, and each pair only lays one egg at a time and can only breed every other year.

Fortunately there are ways to prevent this. The albatrosses can only get at the bait when it is at the surface. Once it has sunk they are not interested because it is too deep for them to dive for. There's a

Great Bustard

Albatrosses may have the greatest wing spans but they're certainly not the heavyweight champions amongst flying birds. The best place to see one of the heavyweight contenders is the village of Villafafilla, a four-hour drive from Madrid in central Spain. We went in early April and on our way to the fields surrounding the village we stopped at Villafafilla's wonderful church tower. An Easter procession was weaving its way through the narrow streets and a peal of church bells announced the time: it was 8 am. The bells themselves, beautiful copper objects with a coating of green verdigris from their years exposed to the weather, didn't announce anything. The pealing was in fact pre-recorded and emanated from a tape recorder in a nearby building. There was a live accompaniment to the taped bells though. Around the top of the tower, there were the stick nests of nine pairs of white storks, and a bird returning to its mate was doing the characteristic stork greeting – throwing back its head and clattering together the upper and lower mandibles of its bright red beak. The birds were used to people, and took no notice of the Easter parade, or a film crew with binoculars watching them from the ground.

The giant birds we'd come here to see probably wouldn't be so obliging. There are 25 species of bustards, all are found in the Old World, 21 of them on the African continent. They inhabit flat open country, sometimes in scrub or light woodland. Most are medium-sized but there are two huge species: the Kori bustard of Africa and the great bustard of Europe. Both can weigh nearly 20 kg (44 lb), as much as a six-year-old child.

Great bustards, the species we had come to film, are notoriously difficult to get close to. Birds of open grasslands have long necks and superb vision and therefore notice predators or anything that doesn't look quite right from a great distance. Filming from a car or on foot was out of the question – the birds would notice us well before even our longest lenses could be trained on them. But there was a solution.

In Europe there are few natural grasslands and great bustards live exclusively on land cleared and worked on by people. The birds are not frightened of tractors or trailers, so that is what we used to get close. Keeping our heads below the metal sides of the trailer, we clanked through the Spanish countryside, bouncing over ploughed fields or along the edges of fields of alfalfa. Somewhere on this patchwork quilt of brown and green, there were around 1,000 great bustards. They are also found in Hungary, Russia and Turkey with smaller numbers in Germany, Switzerland and Austria, but the Spanish population – the country has over 18,000 of them – is the largest in the world. Until the

Left, This is the church in the village of Villafilla in central Spain. White storks circled the bell tower as the Easter parade weaved its way through the streets. It wasn't the storks we had come here to see, however, it was the great bustard. Notoriously difficult to get close to the great bustard inhabits flat open country, and sometimes scrub or light woodland

1830s, droves of great bustards bred in the English countryside around East Anglia, until an increase in arable farming caused their range to contract dramatically. The last recorded breeding took place in Suffolk in 1832 and since then there have been odd vagrants from the Continent.

The farmer knew what we were trying to achieve; he would stop his tractor once we were close to a group of bustards. The trailer was open-topped, so we had a view of the sky which stayed a brilliant hedgesparrow's-egg blue, for the whole day. Other than above our heads, our only view was through a tiny crack between the metal sheets that made up the trailer's sides. I tried to press my eye against this as we were moving but soon had to give up. This was the bumpiest of rides, and without seeing what terrain was coming up, you could never predict when you were going to be bounced into the air. We spent the journey braced in the corners. So that their equipment wouldn't be shaken to pieces, the cameraman lay spread-eagled over his precious camera and lenses and the soundman clutched his tape machine to his chest. After 45 minutes there was a jolt and we stopped. I put my head above the sides of the trailer and realised that our 'Trojan horse' had got us within 30 m (98 ft) of a group of 20 birds.

Similar to turkeys in shape, these giants didn't disappoint. Standing proud against the skyline they were handsome birds indeed. The early morning sunshine enhanced their rich colours, their dark chestnut necks contrasted with their ivory white throats and light grey heads. Their sand-brown backs

Top, A displaying male is an incredible sight. In order to attract a mate he will perform an elaborate display, inflating his neck and splaying his feathers. It is almost as if he turns himself inside-out. Looking like a white ball which can be seen over some distance he will hold this position for 2–3 minutes
Middle, Similar to turkeys in shape the great bustard can weigh up to 20 kg (40 lb) – as much as a six-year old child
Below, Our open-topped trailer managed to get within 30 m (98 ft) of a group of 20 great bustards

had intricate vermiculations of black. Long, white feathers hanging down from either side of the birds' bills, made them look as if they had drooping 'moustaches'. All of these bustards were males in courtship garb. The females are much smaller, two thirds of the height of the 1 m- (3 ft-) tall males and a third of their weight. They are also much drabber, lacking the drooping white feathers around the face, and vivid colours on the neck. They need to be camouflaged because in a month or so they'll choose a patch of bare ground to lay two or three eggs. Single-handedly they incubate the clutch and rear the chicks. First they need to mate. The cock birds are dandies through and through – they put a lot of effort into attracting females, but once they have, their responsibilities are over.

For three days we followed the birds around. You could never predict how the birds would react when our tractor stopped, but for us the parcel to be passed was always the camera. One group of males ignored us completely so we could record how they attract females. It was unbelievable, involving self inflation which makes them look almost as if they have turned themselves inside-out. The birds have no territory but instead there is a lek or display ground, which is dominated by the most powerful males, who perform when and where they please. As I watched, one of the nearest males took up position on a mound of earth. His neck began to expand until it was grossly inflated, which had the effect of splaying out and pointing upwards the long white feathers of his moustaches, partially obscuring his eyes. This trick was done by blowing up the gular pouch, which can be filled with air through an aperture under the tongue, just as I'd seen the maroubou stalks do, but for a different purpose.

As the contortions began, the bird tilted its head backwards, at the same time as lifting his tail over his back until it was actually touching his tilted head. The transformation was finished by twisting over and fanning out the inner feathers of the wing into an elaborate rosette. Any part of his body that was pure white was now brought to the fore, and he stayed in this position for two or three minutes, looking like a snowball on stilts. No sounds accompanied the virtuoso performance in the wide open space. Where bustards are found there is no need, visual signals are enough of an advertisement. A displaying male is a brilliant white ball visible over a considerable distance.

Other bustard flocks that weren't intent on courtship could be very wary. We needed a sequence of these giants actually in flight. This was just as impressive as their courting rituals. The take-off they needed was surprisingly short. They had a yellow undercarriage like the feet of enormous chickens, and if the take off was in low light you see could puffs of soil as they pounded along the ground. Once they were airborne they became ghostly apparitions with pale heads, and with shining white wings they flew with majesty and power. Maybe in the next millennium great bustards will be seen in British airspace again.

Above, It is surprising to think that these large, heavy birds can actually fly, but once airborne they move very gracefully. Their chestnut and white plumage stands out vividly against the sky

Mute Swan

There's another contender for the heaviest flying bird, although it's usually thought of as just a graceful swimmer. One of the most familiar creatures in the world, the mute swan can be found on most gravel pits and reservoirs, on lakes and larger rivers whether these are in the countryside or in a city. It ranges over much of Europe and Asia, notably the United Kingdom, the Netherlands, Denmark, southern Sweden, Germany and Poland. Mute swans have also been introduced to Australia, New Zealand, South Africa and parts of North America.

In the wild, male or cob mute swans commonly weigh in at 14 kg (31 lb), while females or pens grow to about two thirds of this size. Fattened on hand-outs, individuals that live in close contact with people grow even larger. Exceptional individuals reach 18 kg (40 lb). The largest mute swan ever recorded was a cob from Poland that weighed in at 22.5 kg (49 lb 10 oz). The trouble with these really large individuals is that they have probably lost their ability to fly.

Even when they're not overweight, mute swans are probably the laziest fliers of all the swans. Pairs aren't inclined to move very far if they're in a food-rich territory, with plenty of water weeds as well as other aquatic plants with succulent stalks, rhizomes and roots, and frogs, worms, insects and snails, and the possibility of a little supplementary bread or grain from us. There is virtually no migration between Britain and mainland Europe, although a few continental birds may reach our shores during really severe winters. One of the only times mute swans really have to fly is when they first can. The young of the season reach the flying stage in September or October – about 130 days after hatching. From then on families start to break up, the parents usually playing a major part in this. They need to be left alone to prepare for the next breeding season, so they chase their young away from the water on which they were raised. Some broods stay with their parents until the next spring but usually they're driven away during late autumn or winter.

The young birds wander for a while but soon gather in non-breeding flocks. These are crucial to teenage swans, as it is in these groups that cobs and pens pair up. In the majority of cases, the partnership will last for life, unless one of the pair is killed. When the pair are ready to find a breeding territory, usually in their second or third spring, they look for a stretch of river without other swans. In Britain this would usually be a few kilometres long. Lakes, ponds or gravel pits can be good territories too.

We needed to film mute swans taking off, landing and in flight, but this is very unpredictable with pairs or families living alone. One can never know exactly when swans are going to fly. To maximise our chances, we went to one of my favourite places – a lagoon behind a crescent of shingle in Dorset, England. Chesil Beach is a giant in its own right. It is Britain's largest spit, a bank of shingle 12 m (40 ft) high in places, which stretches 16 km (10 miles) from Abbotsbury to the Island of Portland. Behind the beach, there is a brackish lagoon called the Fleet.

At any time of year, this body of water has hundreds of mute swans. In winter when non-breeding birds join the resident population, there can be over 1,000. The

Top right, Mute swans are regarded as the heaviest flying birds. The biggest on record was a male from Poland that weighed 22.5 kg (49 lb 10 oz)

Right, While filming in Dorset I found myself sitting down in the chilly water of the Fleet lagoon, surrounded by mute swans

Fleet is rich in eel grass, a submerged plant mute swans feed on, so a few have probably always been there. Numbers really took off in the 11th Century when Benedictine monks established a colony because fattened cygnets were a delicacy at feasts. Nine hundred years on, cygnets are no longer eaten but there's still a managed swan colony at Abbotsbury, the only one in the world. Because there's a super abundance of food – eel grass and three meals of grain for the swan herd daily – the birds don't need a large territory. They nest in colonies, with pairs sometimes only two swan necks distance apart.

For our filming we followed the weather forecasts closely. We needed a sunny day so that our film would capture the sensational beauty of swans. We wouldn't accept anything less than a blue sky backdrop. We also needed a stiff breeze – a windy day is your best chance of seeing swans being aerobatic – unless that day is in July or August which is moulting time. It takes between 4–7 weeks for the old, worn feathers to be replaced by new ones. During that period swans are flightless.

I never tire of the thrill of seeing swans in flight or getting airborne. Even with its 2 m (7 ft) wingspan and huge paddles for feet, a swan needs a long clear stretch of water to take off. The cameraman and I waited at the lagoon. Floating in front of us there were 100 or so of

Left, Mute swans breed between April and June; 5–7 eggs are laid which take just over a month to hatch. Cygnets were regarded as a delicacy by the Benedictine monks who lived at Abbotsbury in the 10th Century

these huge, sedate birds. Sooner or later one, two or a few of them would fly. While we watched the birds were never quiet. They honked and snorted as they bathed, chased or dabbled for food. 'Mute' swan seems such an inappropriate name, but I suppose they're quieter than the whoopers, our hand-reared ones make a hell of a din. Suddenly without warning, one bird thrust its neck forward, spread its wings and began to push with its feet on the water. Another bird, probably its mate followed suit. Chesil Beach was behind them and it seemed they would need all 16 km (10 miles) of its length to get airborne. Their feet churned up a shimmering spiral of water. It looked so cumbersome but within 30 m (98 ft) the birds were underway. They circled around, a dull white against the gravel spit, becoming brighter – almost luminous white – as they flew, ascending into the blue vault of the sky. Slow, powerful wing-beats brought them right over my head. The flight had a musical accompaniment – their wings produce a magical throbbing whistle. This was only a short circuit; the grain barrow would be wheeled down soon and they landed amongst the flock. That one flight only lasted for 2–3 minutes but it gave us an opportunity for some spectacular filming. It's easy to become blasé about mute swans. They're so abundant and familiar – Britain has about 20,000 pairs. But next time you think 'Oh, it's just another swan', watch them for a while. They swim so proudly, like snow-white galleons, but see how the feathers take on the influences of the light and their surroundings; as they swim under overhanging vegetation they take on the colour of leaves. At dawn, if the sun rises cleanly, the great white birds become pink, while the setting sun turns them a molten orange. Their necks arch gracefully and they are so flexible. Watch how a swan lays its head down on its back, surely the softest of pillows. Above all, try to see a swan unfurl its great wings and fly and marvel that it is one of the heaviest birds that can do that. Swans are giants that allow all of us really close-up views.

Tarantulas

Spiders are possibly the most commonly feared creatures in the world, but this reaction is usually out of all proportion to the danger they actually pose. Tarantulas embody all that is terrifying about spiders: they are hairy, venomous and large. The goliath tarantula for example, can measure up to 25 cm (10 in) in diameter.

It was a late summer's day in the year 1377. The obsessive rhythm of the instruments, particularly the violin and the drum, had been heard for hours. In a trance a young woman swayed slowly from side to side. Then, without warning her body convulsed as if she was held up by invisible strings controlled by a manic puppeteer. Her heavy skirt was made of a rough, heavy material, but her movements were so violent it swirled around her as if it was made of the lightest silk. Her head lolled downwards, and the dusty soil beneath her feet was spattered with drops of sweat from her brow, as if it had started to rain. The she jerked again and continued whirling like a dervish. After six hours her frenzied dance was nearly over. Overcome with exhaustion she sighed and collapsed to the ground. A gaggle of watchers ran forward and gently lifted her onto the back of a cart.

She was unaware of the vines laden with succulent black grapes that she was carried past. She had been picking these fruits when the accident had happened – this is what prompted her frantic dancing. She had been reaching into the light green curtain of vine leaves when she felt a needle-sharp pain in her arm. Recoiling in horror she looked down and saw a shadowy shape disappear into a burrow in the soil at her feet. Surely this was the spider that had bitten her returning to its lair.

The peasants who worked the fields in southern Italy in the Middle Ages believed there was only one cure for the bite of a spider, a dance called the tarantella. They thought that exhausting themselves with a wild and frenzied dance would flush the venom from the body. When she awoke the girl found that the symptoms of dizziness, stomach pains and nausea were gone, the dancing must have done the trick. In truth they would have gone if she'd simply fallen asleep. The province of Taranto in southern Italy was named after the dance and the bristly spider that lived in the burrows in the fields came to be called the 'tarantula'. Since then all big hairy spiders have been given that name. The irony is that the spider in the burrow wasn't the type that bites people and it is not closely related to the big tropical spiders that became its namesake.

It is thought the spider with a venomous bite most likely cause these symptoms was the European black widow; a small, easily-overlooked species that conceals itself in foliage such as vines. The more conspicuous species that the harvesters found and blamed was what we now recognise today as the European wolf spider, about 3 cm (1 in) long, typically grey in colour with darker chevrons on the abdomen and yellow mouth parts. This spider is shy and not aggressive but ground vibrations can sometimes bring

Left, The pink-toed tarantula *Avicularia metallica* is found in Guyana, French Guiana, Brazil, Venezuela and Trinidad. With thick hairy legs the female can grow to 5 cm (2 in) and the male to 3.5 cm (1.5 in)

it to the entrance of its burrow and a fleeting glimpse of this fast-moving creature can be unnerving. In fact it will only bite people if it is squashed or grabbed and our nervous system isn't affected by its venom.

The folklore became so entrenched that when European explorers found huge scary spiders in the tropics, they called them tarantulas too. The European wolf spider belongs to the family Lycosidae; what we all know as tarantulas today belong to a completely different family, the Theraphosidae. The are about 800 species in the group which is fairly primitive. Beneath their heads and huge, prey-crushing jaws they have a pair of large parallel fangs. When they need to bite prey or enemies, these fangs snap open like a pen knife, and stabbed downwards with such force they can sometimes go right through smaller prey items. More advanced spiders have fangs that are arranged opposite one another, these open and close with a 'pincer'

action. Another feature that defines tarantulas is the arrangement at the ends of their eight legs. They have claws which are retractable like a cat's; they are extended when the spider needs to grip onto rough surfaces. The broad, padded feet are always hairy, and the hundreds of thousands of bristles make them adhesive so the spiders can cling to smooth surfaces.

Before the research for *Giants* I'd always imagined tarantulas in the humid rainforests or dry deserts of the Americas, but surprisingly they are found in many parts of the world including the Mediterranean. None are found in southern Italy where the legend and the name started, but small ones of the genus *Ischnocolus* can be found in the olive groves of Spain, Sicily and Morocco. I was also surprised by how beautiful some of the tropical species were, particularly those found in south-east Asia.

Above, The desert or Arizonan blond tarantula is native to this southern state of the USA (as its name suggests) and northern Mexico. The female's large body can measure up to 6 cm (2 in)

Indian Ornamental

The *Poecilotheria* genus includes tarantulas that are stunning. We filmed the mating rituals of the Indian ornamental, a denizen of the forests of southern India and Sri Lanka. It lives under peeling bark or in tree hollows. Females can sometimes have a leg span over 20 cm (7 in); as in all tarantulas the males are smaller. The abdomen is brown, with a bold leaf-like pattern in creamy silver, bordered with black.

The carapace in front of the abdomen is silvery grey with a black centre, underneath the spider has a broad yellow band on the front of the abdomen and bright yellow stripes under the first two pairs of legs. Adult females have banana-yellow undersides. This vivid coloration is flashed when the spider raises the front of its body which it does as a sudden warning to predators. If provoked further it will bring its fangs and venom into play but this is only used as a last resort as venom is a precious resource primarily used for subduing prey.

Tarantulas, like all spiders, have a bizarre sex life. The male Indian ornamental spends its whole life in preparation for mating. Spiders moult their skins as they grow and males will go through a final moult before reaching maturity. In this final stage their behaviour starts to change: rather than hiding behind peeling bark only jumping out to pounce on prey, its sole purpose is now to find and court females.

Male spiders also have special structures used in mating and in this final stage they need to be prepared. These small, slender, leglike structures at the front of their heads are called palps. Typically these are used as an aid during feeding, but in mature male spiders they become swollen into conspicuous bulbs, like boxing gloves. Inside each one there is an embolus, a highly unusual copulatory organ. Nothing comparable exists in the animal kingdom.

The male tarantula then constructs a sheet of dense silk above ground level. Crawling beneath this he turns over on his back to deposit sperm on the web. He then moves above the web and reaches underneath to insert his swollen palps into the sperm droplets. They siphon up the sperm like the bulb in a fountain pen filter. The process can take a number of hours to complete, and males at the height of their sexual activity can spin two or three sperm webs in a week, whether they've had a chance to mate or not. Now he has the dangerous task of getting close enough to a female to discharge his palps, as she will consider him to be potential prey.

We filmed as a male Indian ornamental slowly climbed the tree towards the female's hole. In tarantula courtship good vibrations are crucial. He must identify himself as a suitor, not as a meal or an enemy, and to do this he began to tap and vibrate his legs on the rough bark of the vertical trunk. As the female sensed the male's approach we saw her leave the dark recesses of her hole and splay out her elegant black, white and grey legs around the entrance. Now the male was drumming a mesmerising beat and from a short distance away I could even hear it myself.

The larger female suddenly erupted out of her retreat straight towards the male but she stopped short and began to tap her own palps on the bark! He drummed even more frantically in response and advanced towards her.

If all had gone well he would have lifted her up with his front legs before introducing each of his swollen palps alternately into a fold under her abdomen, discharging sperm each time. Then he would have made a run for it, as straight after mating is the most likely time for the female to attempt to eat him, but in this case the female wasn't receptive and he had bolted as soon as their legs had touched. He would have to find a female a little more interested in mating.

Left, Attractively marked the fringed ornamental tarantula makes a popular pet. *Poecilotheria ornata* is found in the forests of southern India and Sri Lanka

Far left, Another *Poecilotheria* species is the Salem ornamental or cat-leg tarantula (*P. formosa*). It makes its home in tree cavities

131

Earth Tiger

Not all tarantulas are arboreal, just as many live at ground level. In south-east Asia these species that frequent burrows in the ground are called earth tigers, most belong to the genus *Haplopelma*. The tiger part of their name comes from the fact that they are quick to assume a threat posture with legs raised and fangs bared. They can get so stirred up that they will rear right up, falling onto their backs still continuing to threaten. This display makes them look very formidable indeed but as with all tarantulas they are reluctant to actually attack.

My experience with these culminated in an extraordinary tea party near Chiang Mai in northern Thailand. When it comes to Thai cuisine, most people are familiar with Tom Yam Goong, a fiery concoction of prawns, lemon grass and chillies served in coconut milk, which can clear blocked sinuses more effectively than any nasal spray. However, in a remote region of northern Thailand, the inhabitants of the Lahu hill-tribe prefer something a little more exotic.

Two hours out of Chiang Mai, in the foothills of the Himalayas, the countryside rapidly transforms from flat, featureless plains into lush hillside terraces,

multi-tiered wedding cakes of cultivated rice and corn. Working in these fields is arduous, as the land is still farmed by hand, and the toil is not made any easier by extreme heat and humidity. Out here it's easy to work up a hunger, but luckily for the Lahu, they know where they can bag a quick snack.

I followed one elder and his grandson up through the terraces, my boots becoming evermore weighty with clods of the sticky, fertile soil. Stopping to catch my breath, and let a torrent of sweat pour down my back, I looked out across the valley which was cloaked in a low mist rising from the surrounding forest, towards the Lahus's village of Ban Meung Noi, a

Left, In a remote region of northern Thailand we visited the Lahu hill-tribe. Here they grow rice and corn on lush, hill-side terraces, but the work is done by hand, a task made more difficult by the heat and humidity in this part of the world

haphazard collection of houses on stilts ringing with the sounds of dogs, chickens and pigs. Meanwhile my companions' eyes were fixed firmly on the ground in front of them, parting the long grass with a casual sweep of their razor-sharp machetes. They were on the look out for small golf ball-sized burrows, home to one of the species belonging to the genus *Haplopelma*. Covered entirely in glossy black hair, this species reaches almost 13 cm (5 in) in diameter.

As we made our way to the edge of a cornfield, the old man suddenly spotted a burrow, hollowed into the side of a gentle slope. The entrance was blocked by a tapestry of silk, leaves and twigs, indicating the presence of a spider. Carefully, clearing the surrounding grass, the old man used his machete to cut around the burrow, without damaging the web. Using the knife now as a spade, he dug down 45 cm (18 in) clearing away the soil, whilst his 12 year old grandson crouched next to him with hollow sections of bamboo

slung over his shoulder, like arrow quivers. A dark leg quivered in the milk-chocolate earth, then another, and another until the whole tarantula was revealed. It nervously scrutinised around the area, trapped in its own lair. Unsure of where to run, it headed straight for the security of a dark tunnel and directly into the bamboo container laid down by the boy. Jamming a leaf into the opening of the bamboo, the boy returned the container to a string of others dangling over his shoulder, each one bearing the same leafy plug.

Dusk was descending as we arrived back at the village, and the cacophony of farmyard noises had now been replaced by grasshoppers and cicadas whispering from the shadows of the forest. The delicate aroma of woodsmoke greeted me as I made my way to the old man's house. Through the shuttered windows I glimpsed golden hues of light splashed onto rough adobe walls and the orchestra of night-life outside was now joined by the erratic percussion of fire crackling,

Above, A stunning south-east Asian species, the cobalt blue tarantula is found in Burma, Cambodia and Thailand. Out in the open the spider's legs become a bright, metallic blue due to a covering of hollow hairs which diffuse the light

sending smoke and ash into the thatched eaves above. Leaving my boots alongside a sea of sandals at the door, I entered the house to find most of the village crouched around the campfire. The large, spacious room served as the kitchen, living room, dining room and master bedroom, and behind the men circling the fire, on a gigantic wooden bed, sat their wives and daughters, adorned in the bold Lahu tones of red and black.

Khun Winai, my local guide and interpreter invited me to sit between him and a man who obviously had never heard of dental hygiene. His teeth looked like they had been brushed with black tar, although I am sure that a brush was the last thing he had ever considered. Besel nut chewing is still extremely popular in this part of Asia, despite the rather unflattering side-effect it produces of stained teeth. Besel nut is used for much the same reasons as cigarettes. When chewed with other plant ingredients it produces a mild calming effect.

Removing the leaf from one of the bamboo quivers, Winai tapped a hand on the other end and out popped the spider. However, before this spider could get very far, Winai deftly picked it up by the thorax and placed it directly into the white hot embers. For a few short

Above, A tea party Lahu-style. I didn't know what I had let myself in for!

Above right, After the spider had been released from its bamboo 'cage' Winai deftly picked it up by the thorax and placed it directly into the white hot embers of the fire

Left, Once the spider has been placed on the fire it is soon consumed by the flames. Here Winai is patting it to remove all the hairs from the body and legs

moments the tarantula scurried frantically about on top of the coals, until eventually it gave up, its body emitting a sizzling hiss and culminating in a bubble-gum pop. Charred and cindered, Wirai patted the body to remove any remaining hairs before breaking off a leg in the same way as one would eat a crab. Here though the whole leg is eaten, nothing is wasted. The taste is apparently half-way between barbecued chicken and crab, although being a vegetarian I had to take Wirai's word for it. Unlike chicken though, where there is always a fight to see who gets a drumstick, with a tarantula there's a leg for everyone. The best is saved until last. With a resounding crunch Mr Besel nut devoured the body, his mouth resembling something out of a horror film, with mangled tarantula body parts poking out from between a mass of stained teeth and bright red gums. As more spiders continued to be put on the fire I sipped my tea nervously and wondered what on earth there would be for dessert.

The south-east Asian species show surprising diversity in colour and form which can be found in tarantulas. In the shade the cobalt blue *Haplopelma lividum*, a Burmese species, is pretty nondescript with a grey body and dark limbs. When viewed out in the sun, however, the legs become a bright, metallic blue due to a covering of hollow hairs which diffuse the light. I found these species breathtakingly beautiful, but they were not really large enough to qualify as giants. In order to see those I would have to travel to Africa and South America.

Below, Saving the best until last. I was told that the taste is half-way between barbecued chicken and crab – and there are enough legs for everyone!

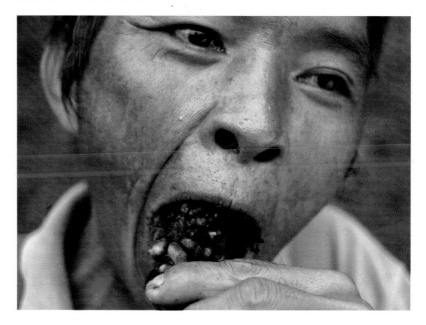

King Baboon

First I went to Africa, to the thorny acacia scrub growing in hard-baked red laterite soil, the favoured habitat of the legendary king baboon tarantula, *Citharischius crawshayi*, a tarantula with a body that can measure up to 15 cm (6 in) long, and a leg span of 20 cm (8 in) or more. Stout rear legs as thick as pencils add to the impression of an enormous size.

A troop of baboons delicately picked seeds and small insects from the grass as I passed. When I have asked people why spiders, particularly tarantulas, are in their top ten least favourite creatures, they usually reply that it is because they have long hairy legs, they can run fast and they can bite you. Baboons and Irish wolf hounds also have these attributes but it is always the invertebrates that get the bad press. Perhaps this is because their form and way of life are so different from our mammalian one. The king baboon spider is named after the primate because the stout hairy legs resemble the fingers of a baboon; the 'king' is simply a reference to their size.

I found a burrow on sloping ground; retreats on an incline are normal for tarantulas so their homes don't fill up with water every time it rains. After storms the king baboons in a population near Voi Kenya are often seen wandering about after being washed out of their subterranean retreats.

Peering into the burrow which was about 10 cm (4 in) across I could see no sign of life. If it was inhabited, I'd have to coax the tarantula to the surface. The grasslands of Africa are sweet and succulent if you happen to enjoy eating grass and a chewed stalk also doubles as a fishing rod for tarantulas. I gently pushed the stem into the hole, wiggling it slightly and I had a bite. Exerting a gentle pressure, I pulled slowly until the king baboon was visible in the entrance with its jaws clamped firmly on the grass. With a quick tug I dragged it into the sunshine.

It was a gorgeous creature with a pelt of bright orange. The densely-packed hair made it appear as if it was covered in crushed velvet. This huge specimen, as big as my hand was a female, so queen baboon would perhaps be a more appropriate name for the species. The males are small in comparison – about half the size – after the final moult at maturity they lose their robust appearance and have long slim legs. They look so different that it used to be thought that they were a separate species.

Understandably, the tarantula wasn't too happy about being dragged out of her home by her teeth and she showed her displeasure. Rubbing her legs together she made an extraordinary chirping noise, using this technique the spider was attempting to scare off the enemy – me. To exaggerate the threat the spider then reared right up on her thick back legs, hissing loudly. I didn't get too close as the 1 cm (0.5 in) fangs were bared and under this much provocation the spider can strike like a cobra. This bite would be painful but tarantulas are certainly not dangerous or lethal to humans as most of us think (unless I happened to be allergic to the venom, but this can be the case with bee venom). I used my grass stem fishing rod to guide the spider back to its burrow, outside in the hot sun it would soon desiccate and would also be vulnerable to predators. Birds as well as mammals prey on tarantulas.

There is some controversy about whether king baboons are the continent's largest spider and there's a tantalising possibility that the African goliath tarantula, *Hysterocrates hercules* from Niger is the biggest or even the world's greatest giant spider, in terms of weight. In 1895, King Koko of Niger sent a letter to Queen Victoria after a revolt, 'We are now very sorry indeed about the killing and eating of parts of your employees. We now throw ourselves entirely at the mercy of the good old queen'.

Above, When the king baboon is threatened she adopts this pose and makes a loud hissing noise. In this situation her fangs are best avoided although the venom is not dangerous to humans

Right, With a thick covering of densely-packed hair the body of the female king baboon looks as if it is covered in crushed velvet

A British gun boat was despatched immediately to rescue the British traders. A Lieutenant Abaohe was part of the mission who returned with a new species of huge spider. The massive body is still preserved in the Natural History Museum in London, but no 'valid' specimens of this enormous species have been located in the field since this discovery over 100 years ago. For now, the crown for the world's largest spider belongs to the South American tarantula and to find this a film crew and I travelled to a rain forest near Cayenne, the capital of French Guiana.

Goliath

My guide in South America was Rick West, a tarantula expert, who had recently found four undescribed species in French Guiana. Amazonia has the greatest diversity of tarantulas; half the known species are found there. We stayed at Emerald Jungle Lodge where Rick seemed to know every tarantula individually. On our first night (tarantulas are usually only active at night) we started by filming a medium-sized, arboreal species with about a 13 cm (5 in) leg span, the pink-toe *Avicularia metallica*. If any spider can be cuddly, this one is. An adult lived on the wooden beams just outside the dining room. In the torchlight its legs and carapace had a blue green sheen, the abdomen was covered in a dense black fur like moleskin, and most delightful of all, each of the eight legs had an ankle sock of pink.

Out in the rain forest we found other, smaller pink-toes and we were able to film a behaviour that was very unexpected. If they were startled, the spiders reminded me of small furry monkeys with the adroit way they launched themselves from a leaf or twig, sailing through the air to another perch or amazingly, if they were above a pool or stream, diving into the water to swim away. They are able to do a stroke that reminded me of the butterfly for short distances, but cannot stay submerged for long because their hairy bodies become waterlogged.

When they are small another handsome species shares the high life with the pink-toes, but once the skeleton tarantula, *Ephebopus murinus*, becomes an adult it lives in burrows on the forest floor. A medium-sized one outside the lodge's kitchen found the spout of a watering can was the best of both worlds: not right on the ground so flying insects would be excluded from its menu, and not so high up (it was also right next to a wall) that it was out of reach of crawling insects.

Rick showed us the burrows of the magnificent adults in the rain forest. The entrances had funnel-shaped silken portals, fragments of leaves and twigs were incorporated into these and the overall effect was of an elegant design. Moving slowly you could approach closely enough to see the legs of the occupants, sometimes the whole spider laying on the silken porch waiting to pounce on any passing insect. The spider gets its name from the yellow stripes along its black legs which really to give the impression of a skeleton costume you might see at fancy dress party with the bones crudely painted onto black fabric.

These spiders were all within walking distance of Emerald Jungle Lodge but for the real object of our quest we had to go to the Réserve Naturelle Trésor, a sopping area of lowland rainforest with trees that reach 45 m (148 ft) into the sky, a total of 1,400 species of plants and the world's greatest spiders, the Goliath tarantula *Theraphosa blondi*. This species is found in Surinan Brazil, Guyana, Venezuela as well as French Guiana, but the largest ever caught was found very close to where we were searching on the Montagne la Gabrielle in 1923. This record breaker had a 25 cm (10 in) leg span and weighed 50 g (2 oz).

The crew filmed Rick and I slipping and sliding down a steep muddy slope, far below us the distant sound of

running water emanated from the valley bottom. Goliath tarantulas prefer to inhabit sloping ground so they don't get flooded out of their burrows and moist areas near water because of an abundance of food. When fully-grown these impressive tarantulas prey mainly on frogs. We'd shot a sequence of a goliath tarantula pouncing on a large cockroach on a set back in England. That was an impressive enough feat, but spiders are predators that can only eat liquid food, so an amphibian would have to be transformed to a half-digested soup outside the tarantula's body before consumption could begin.

In the wild the goliath tarantula would lurk in the entrance of its burrow or just outside, if a frog wandered nearly the spider would strike. After the hollow fangs were embedded, venom would squirt down a fine tube to paralyse the prey. Once subdued, this only takes a few moments, the frog would be dragged back into the tarantula's burrow. Feeding at the surface makes it more vulnerable, and more importantly the odour of the prey would soon attract irritating ants ready to carve up their share of the feast.

Inside the burrow the spider vomits fluid onto the prey, and this aided by the squeezing action of the palps and jaws, causes the frog to begin to come apart. The spider then pauses for a while, and to hold its meal together it parcels up the disintegrating body with silk. Just inside the mouth there is a muscular chamber, the pharynx, and behind that the powerful sucking stomach. These begin to suck the dissolving tissue of the frog inside. Only small morsels can be imbibed; larger ones are filtered out by bristles bordering the mouth, and by the pharynx which has walls with microscopic perforations, and acts like a colander holding larger particles back. With such a large meal the spider may silk the remains three or four times before the process of digestion is over. By then, the prey mass has been reduced to a small pellet of indigestible material.

Goliath tarantulas like all giant spiders are fastidious about cleanliness. Cleaning themselves up after dinner is particularly important. They must rid themselves of pieces of food caught in their mouth parts and they do this in a remarkable way by squirting

Above, The Goliath is also known as the bird-eating spider. This is hardly accurate as although some of these spiders live in trees, they rarely catch birds. The misnomer arose from a painting by a Swiss naturalist published in 1705 which showed a giant spider eating a humming bird. The only time these spiders are likely to kill and eat birds is when they are young; it is extremely unlikely that they could catch and kill fit, adult birds

a stream of digestive fluid back out through the pharynx and mouth. This lifts off any particles still adhering so they can be wiped away by the palps or legs. Tarantulas even use squirts of gastric juices to groom themselves, pulling their legs across their mouth parts and using the liquid to dislodge soil particles and the like, so these can be rubbed off easily.

Knowing all this I couldn't wait to meet this spider that hunted frogs in the wild. Rick pointed to a burrow in a muddy bank. The entrance looked huge; goliath tarantulas often modify the burrows of agoutis – forest rats, rodents that are by no means small. On my hands and knees and using a flashlight, I could see the spider wasn't that far in; as if it was shy, its face was covered by brown hairy legs.

Mark Yates set up his camera, Mark Roberts attached his microphone to his boom pole. We were now ready to film my encounter with the world's largest spider. Breaking off a twig, Rick gently inserted it into the hole. This was a threat to the spider and she launched an attack, throwing herself at the offending object. The momentum took her to the burrow entrance and ultimately right out onto the forest floor.

She was a gorgeous creature, her heavy body covered in a pelt of chocolate brown hair. Many South American species of tarantula have an unusual mode of

defence and we filmed as this began to take place. I thought I was far enough away not to be affected by the tarantulas defensive weapon but I was wrong. With rapid movements, the spider stroked its back legs over its abdomen unleashing a barrage of thousands of urticating hairs. We filmed a stream of them floating through the air. These hairs are a formidable weapon against mammalian predators; their design allows them to penetrate flesh and cause inflammation and pain, particularly in the eyes, that can last for weeks, as I found to my cost. Even though I was at least 1 m (3 ft) away, a few hairs were thrown far enough to embed themselves in my eyelids. I tried not to rub my eyes as this can do more damage by pushing into an upright position any hairs that were lying flat on my skin and lodging them further in. Even taking this precaution and washing my face with water as soon as I could, some hairs were still anchored into my flesh; they have hooks and barbs and for the next week or so my eyelids were puffy and sore.

Of course in the heat of the moment, I didn't even think about hairs and the irritation, the spider was too awe-inspiring. Even with their battery of defences, they have a painful bite too, goliath tarantulas are not invulnerable. Small tarantulas of any species are eaten by anything large enough to swallow them. In the rain

Above Unlike the goliath the pink-toed tarantula really does eat birds. The goliath lives on the ground which makes preying on birds difficult. The pink-toe, however, lives in trees which gives them a perfect vantage point for catching birds

forests adults are attacked and killed by raccoon-like, brown-nosed coati and predaceous birds such as the trumpeter.

Closer scrutiny of my first goliath tarantula revealed it was being fed on already, but to a lesser, non-lethal degree. A cluster of what looked like thin, white hairs were attached to an indentation on top of her carapace. These were the egg shells of a tiny acricerid fly. On hatching, the maggots had crawled to the side of the carapace, puncturing areas of thin cuticles, to feed off the spider's body fluids. Rick said that most goliaths he found carried these parasites.

As Rick gently guided the spider back to its burrow, it hissed loudly, I knew king baboons stridulated but I didn't realise goliath tarantulas did it too. Eventually the great spider disappeared into her burrow. She would spend most of her life underground spending as little time as possible at the surface, only appearing there when she was grabbing prey, or finding a new burrow after she'd outgrown her old one or perhaps been washed out of it.

Goliath tarantulas were quite frequent in the forest and we found five or six more within 10 m (33 ft) of the first. We continued looking as some of the holes could have a white ball in the entrance which was something I really hoped we could film.

About ten months after mating, female goliath tarantulas lay 80–120 eggs (other species can lay about 1,000 in rapid succession, completing the process in 30 minutes or so). Then she spins a blanket of fine silk gathering up the corners to roll the eggs inside it. She will carry this tennis-ball sized parcel, holding on with her palps and legs, for the next two or three months. Most tarantulas carry their eggs around in this way, although some *Pterinochilus* species from Africa lay their eggs in a silk package, with ends twisted like a sweet wrapper suspended in a labyrinth of silk. African species such as the feathery baboon *Stomatopelma grisipes* attaches its egg sac to a pad of hard silk on the trunk of a tree.

Goliath tarantulas, like many tarantulas, lavish great affection on their egg masses. To prevent the eggs at the bottom getting crushed by the others, they regularly turn the silken sac so pressure doesn't build up unequally. They also heat their eggs in the sun – the behaviour we wanted to film – pushing the egg mass to the mouth of their burrow and slowly revolving it so the developing spiderlings are warmed equally.

Once the eggs hatch the babies moult once inside their silken ball. Too weak to escape themselves they rely on their mother to free them. They stay with her in the burrow, nourished by their yolk sacs until they moult again. Once they've done this, the very hairy, greyish black spiderlings, about 30 mm (1 in) in diameter, disperse and begin to feed themselves. A few species of tarantula take this maternal care even further; the young cluster around their mother's mouth parts while she regurgitates a nutritive fluid for them, rather like pigeon squabs getting pigeon milk from their parents.

Unfortunately, we didn't find a mother warming its egg mass as we'd hoped, but we did find something else – a hollow but exact replica of a goliath spider complete with hairs, fangs, mouth parts, legs, and carapace – a cast skin. When tarantulas outgrow their old skins, special stretch receptors tell them when they are bulging, and the moult begins. This remarkable process can take up to eight hours with the spider moving body fluids around to break out. It begins with the spider rolling over on its back. The cuticle that surrounds its body has already lost some of its rigidity, so that when the spider pumps body fluids the hydraulic pressure cracks its exoskeleton open. To create extra strain it jiggles its mouth parts too. The carapace finally cracks open, and it lifts off completely, like the lid of a tin can.

Once the same process has split open the abdomen the tricky part begins; the new legs must be extricated from the old cast. Once the first couple are free, then they are used to help pull out the rest. For a while the legs hang limply but then they're bent abruptly and flexed gymnastically, this probably stretches the joints so they remain flexible while the cuticle is hardening. It takes up to a week for the new covering to harden fully and the spider doesn't risk injuring itself by hunting during this time, but after that it begins to feed and grow once more.

The sight of this cast skin brought home to me that there will never be a definitive tarantula record breaker. There is of course an absolute size limit imposed on how much an exoskeleton can support, but I am sure the champion tarantulas found so far haven't reached that ceiling. They never stop growing throughout their life so new record breakers are out there. On our walk through that forest in French Guiana we could have been sensed by a goliath tarantula more gigantic than any that have been found before.

Species index

a

Aardvark 21, 23
Agouti 140
Albatross, royal 116, 117
Albatross, shy 116
Albatross, wandering 116, 117, 118, 119
Albatross, waved 116
Anaconda, green 13, 26, 27, 28
Anteater, giant 27
Antelope, Buffon's kob 19
Antelope, roan 19
Avicularia metallica 128, 138

b

Bandicoot, golden 88
Bat, Egyptian fruit 18
Bear, American black 57, 60, 62, 63, 64, 65, 66, 70, 76
Bear, Asiatic black 59
Bear, brown 57, 66, 67, 68, 69, 70, 76
Bear, grizzly 57, 67
Bear, Malayan sun 58
Bear, polar 57, 70, 72, 73, 74, 75, 76, 77, 78, 79, 80, 81
Bear, sloth 59
Bear, spectacled 59
Bee eater 18
Bettong 88
Boa constrictor 13
Boa, common 13
Brachypelma smithi
Buffalo, water 96, 97
Bustard, great 120, 122, 123
Bustard, Kori 120

c

Caiman 27, 28
Capybara 27, 28
Cassowary, dwarf 104
Cassowary, single wattled 104
Cassowary, southern 104
Citharischius crawshayi 136, 137
Cobra, king 13
Condor, Andean 112, 113, 115, 116, 117
Condor, Californian 115
Copepods 41
Crocodile, Nile 13

d

Deer, Rusa 96
Duck, whistling 27

e

Emu 104, 105
Ephebopus murinus 138

g

Goose, snow 102

h

Haplopelma lividum 132, 133, 135
Honeyeater, Lewin's 104
Honeyeater, yellow-gaped 104

Hysterocrates hercules 136

i

Ibis, glossy 27

j

Jacana, wattled 28

k

Kingfisher, white-tailed 104
Kiwi 104
Komodo dragon 94, 95, 96, 97, 98, 99

l

Latrodectus mactans 128, 129
Lizard, common 84
Lizard, eyed 85
Lizard, sand 84

m

Monitor, black-headed 85
Monitor, crocodile 92
Monitor, Gray's 91
Monitor, perentie 86, 87, 88, 89, 91, 97
Monitor, pygmy 86
Monitor, water 90, 91

o

Ostrich 104, 105, 106, 107

p

Panda, giant 58, 59, 68
Petrel, providence 116
Poecilotheria formosa 131
Poecilotheria ornata 131
Poecilotheria regalis 130
Porcupine 14
Python, African rock 13, 18, 19, 20, 21, 22, 23
Python, amethystine 13, 17
Python, Burmese (golden) 14, 15, 16
Python, Indian 13
Python, reticulated 13, 24, 25, 26

r

Rat, cane 20
Remora 37

s

Salmon, pacific 68, 69
Sea lion 49
Seal, fur 50, 51, 52
Seal, harp 80
Seal, hooded 80
Seal, ringed 79, 80
Shark, basking 36, 38, 39
Shark, blacktip reef 32, 33, 46
Shark, blue 46
Shark, bonnethead 45
Shark, Caribbean reef 32, 33, 46
Shark, great hammerhead 44, 45
Shark, great white 31, 45, 48, 49, 50, 51, 52, 53, 54, 55
Shark, Greenland sleeper 40, 41, 42, 43

Shark, lemon 46
Shark, mako 36
Shark, megamouth 36, 38
Shark, oceanic whitetip 33, 46
Shark, Pacific sleeper 43
Shark, pygmy 33
Shark, scalloped hammerhead 45
Shark, smooth hammerhead 45
Shark, tiger 45, 46
Shark, whale 31, 34, 36, 37
Shark, winghead 44
Sheltopusik 85
Slow worm 84
Snake, European whip 13
Snake, glass 85
Snake, king 13
Snake, rat 13
Spider, European Black Widow 128, 129
Spider, European Wolf 128, 129
Starling 102
Stingray 28
Stork, jabiru 27
Stork, marabou 102, 108, 109, 110, 111, 112, 116, 117, 23
Stork, white
Swan, mute 102, 124, 125
Swan, trumpeter 102
Swan, whooper 102

t

Tarantula, African goliath 136
Tarantula, Arizonan blond 129

Tarantula, cobalt blue 132, 133, 135
Tarantula, fringed ornamental 131
Tarantula, goliath 127, 139, 140, 141
Tarantula, Indian ornamental 130, 131
Tarantula, king baboon 136, 137
Tarantula, pink-toed 128, 138
Tarantula, Salem ornamental 131
Tarantula, skeleton 138
Theraphosa blondi 127, 138, 139, 140, 141
Trevally, golden 37
Turtle, flat-back 87
Turtle, freshwater 27
Turtle, green 87

v

Viper, gaboon 13

w

Wallaby, hare 88
Wallaroo 88
Whale, beluga 80
Whale, killer 48
White pointer (see shark, great white above)

Picture credits